"The World According to
Manager 01/02"

By David Black

© Ronnie Dog Media 2017

This book is dedicated to all of those that lost hours, days, weeks, months or even years of their lives playing this game.

Follow me on Twitter: @cm9798

www.cm9798.co.uk

Foreword

"You should have done 2001/02. That was the best one for me."

There are only so many times you can hear that before a cartoon lightbulb appears above your head and you decide that maybe there is something to it after all.

I didn't envisage writing one book, let alone two, and whilst I'm hardly JK Rowling I am more than a little relieved that the first book received a largely positive reaction. If you did buy it, thank you! It warms my heart that as of this writing, it has 4.5 stars out of 5 on Amazon. From 10 reviews! Not one of them is a family member, which is something I've had words about...

Anyway, the lightbulb moment occurred in March when I was at my day job and a client visited our offices. Clients are given a tour which includes our display wall, where members of staff contribute weird and wonderful things to give the office a bit of character. Amongst these items is my literary work. The client was given the office tour, passing the display wall and arriving at my desk a few minutes later. I didn't expect the following sentence:

"So you're the Championship Manager man? I still love it, I was up all night playing 01/02!"

To be very honest, when I started www.cm9798.co.uk (there's that plug again) in January 2015 I was in two minds. There was no doubt CM01/02 was the more popular game and had quite a web presence already, which is why I chose 97/98 as my game to blog. I don't regret that, as I can make a case for both games being my favourite, but now I basically want to have my cake and eat it.

When the game was current, you couldn't get me off it. It had network facilities which meant I could play with friends without having to leave my house, and that counts as socialising, right? I had two particular CM network buddies who are very much at opposite ends of the spectrum. Firstly a chap called Rob, who I've never met in person but I must have spent 5 hours a day losing to him during school holidays, but also Steve, who has had to put up with me since we were 11 and was best man at my wedding. This book is for all the Rob's and Steve's out there who lost days to the flashing text.

I must thank a few people who have made book two a reality. Firstly my good friend Paul for giving up his own time to proof read my nonsense and offer helpful hints & facts along the way. Your support (and memory!) has been invaluable and I only hope that one day I can return the favour to you. Editor-in-Chief Chris Darwen continues to give me opportunities in the writing world and perhaps worryingly for him seems to think my ideas are mostly good ones. Your enthusiasm for my work goes a long way but not as far as giving me a platform to be published on, and for that I can only be grateful.

My wife Steph is probably the world's most tolerant person, putting up with my football obsession is a task in itself but encouraging me further by giving me license to have a man cave which you then beautifully decorated whilst I wrote this book is well beyond the call of wifely duties. It really must be love. Thank you for helping me achieve my dreams.

With that, let's head back to 2001. I hope you enjoy this to the tune of at least 4.5 stars

David Black (@cm9798)
November 2017

Introduction

For those of you who read the first book, you might be relieved to find this isn't a sequel. Forget everything you remember about my England side losing in the semi-finals of World Cup 1998, for the purposes of this book it didn't happen. I'm prepared for Kevin Pilkington to give up his fictional England cap. If you haven't read the first book, treat yourself and order it. Tell your friends. Give it a 5 star review. Then forget it and read this book.

I've moved on to Championship Manager 01/02. Without giving you the whole history of the series, CM01/02 is the fourth and final version of the CM3 series (CM9798 was the final version of the CM2 series, for those keeping score). It means it is the most polished and, in many people's view, the best version of the game in the series. The next game released in the series would be CM4, which saw the debut of the 2D pitch, so we're still on scrolling text here. CM01/02 is so popular there are still new databases being released even now, whether it be current day updates or a database for the 89/90 season. They aren't the only ones, the internet is full of people's good work.

The game is available as freeware as of 2008, which certainly helped maintain the popularity, especially as it is readily available to download. But where CM01/02 really shines is the list of cult players you can find within. There are several players in the database who are nothing short of legends in the game, eleven of whom feature on the cover art of this book. By now everybody knows of To Madeira being fictional, Cherno Samba sadly not being the goal machine he was made out to be and Mark Kerr not going on to win the Champions League, but we didn't know back then and that's what makes it great.

A patch was made available shortly after release in 2001 which tidied up some of the in game issues and database errors (including our favourite Portugese striker) but I'm having none of that. I've installed the out of the box version which I've still kept hold of to this day and we're going to embrace it.

I can already hear my Dad saying that he is confused and we haven't even kicked a metaphorical ball yet, so let's move on to the state of play in July 2001. Manchester United are the undoubted favourites for the Premier League, having won three consecutive titles and will be hot favourites to make it four in a row having signed Juan Veron and Ruud van Nistelrooy for a combined fee of approximately £47m. In reality, the signing of the latter lead to the demise of the

Cole & Yorke partnership that had proved to be prolific, but here Sir Alex Ferguson has all three at his disposal. Speaking of Fergie, before the season began he announced his decision to retire at the end of the 2001/02 season, a decision he later reversed as his career went on to span more than another decade. One potential issue for the Red Devils is that star defender Jaap Stam has been sold to Lazio and replaced by 35 year old Laurent Blanc, presumably just so he can perform the head kissing ritual with Barthez.

Arsenal have managed to be runners-up for three consecutive seasons, which although is ridiculous I think Gunners fans would take that in the modern day. In 2000/01, Arsenal finished 10 points behind Man Utd and lost 6-1 at Old Trafford, which was seemingly the trigger point for Arsene Wenger to get the chequebook out over the summer. Despite spending £28m on the likes of Francis Jeffers, Giovanni van Bronckhorst, Richard Wright and Junichi Inamoto, the most eyebrow-raising signing of the summer was Sol Campbell joining for free from rivals Tottenham Hotspur. Could Campbell be the centre half they need to bridge that gap? Well, it certainly helped in real life as they went on to secure a league and cup double, so let's see if Sports Interactive rate Sol just as highly.

Liverpool, under Gerard Houllier, have enjoyed success on just about all fronts but the Premier League still alludes them. With Fowler, Owen, Heskey and Litmanen as striking options, it is perhaps no surprise that they've signed two goalkeepers in Jerzy Dudek and Chris Kirkland to try and tighten up at the other end. Left back John Arne Riise has also joined to replace the departed Christian Ziege. Whilst the title might be a step too far, they'll be confident of securing a Champions League spot which has extended to the top four for the first time.

They'll face a challenge from a few teams on that front, with pre-Abramovich Chelsea still spending plenty as they shelled out £11m to bring Frank Lampard across London from West Ham. I think it's fair to say that was good business. William Gallas joins a very young John Terry and a much older Marcel Desailly at the back, whilst £15m buys you Emmanuel Petit and Boudewijn Zenden. Zola, Hasselbaink & Gudjohnsen are a good set of strikers to call upon. Also in the Champions League mix are Leeds United, who have an exciting young team captained by Rio Ferdinand alongside the likes of Mark Viduka, Harry Kewell, Robbie Keane and Lee Bowyer. They are just about pre-financial meltdown here, and who knows, if they qualify for the Champions League, they might just avoid it.

Newcastle United were the surprise package of the season, having finished mid-table in the previous 4 seasons. However, Sir Bobby Robson had been in charge since 1999 and with his appointment came stability, and by 2001 a promising team had been assembled, with former England captain Alan Shearer leading the side. Ably supported by the experienced Gary Speed, Rob Lee and Shay Given, the signings of Craig Bellamy and Laurent Robert to join the likes of Kieron Dyer and Nolberto Solano made the Magpies quite the attacking unit on their day. Robson had talked of pushing for the top 8 but momentum can take you a long way in football…

Elsewhere, the three promoted clubs are North West duo Blackburn and Bolton, alongside Fulham, bankrolled by Mohamed Al-Fayed. Despite it being Fulham's debut season, an outlay of £34m meant they were never likely to struggle and were even tipped to push for the European places at the season's start. Bolton, managed by Sam Allardyce, have more of a workmanlike approach and bravely stuck with the majority of the squad that earned promotion, though this would change as the season wore on. Here though they have to rely on Rod Wallace and Dean Holdsworth to score the goals to keep them afloat. Blackburn are managed by Graeme Souness, with the standout players being Damien Duff and Matt Jansen. Rovers actually went on to win the League Cup in this season in reality, but they'll be hard pushed to repeat that success here.

Sunderland had come agonisingly close to securing European football the previous season, and with European Golden Boot winner Kevin Phillips forming a potent striker force with veteran Niall Quinn, the outlook was positive for the new season. Peter Reid bolstered his striking options with the capture of Frenchman Lillian Laslandes but would it be enough to push the Black Cats up the table? Also pushing the top 6 are Aston Villa, who are managed by John Gregory. Gregory lasted until January in the real world but can he last any longer here? Their main summer move was replacing David James with Peter Schmeichel, which would surely only help their cause. They also spent £5.8m on Croatian forward Bosko Balaban in a bid to boost their goals for column. As it turned out, Schmeichel would outscore Balaban...

Charlton found themselves perennially in mid-table during this era, and to this day nobody can explain how. It is probably a testament to the skills of manager Alan Curbishley. It is a squad with few star names but young striker Jason Euell is the best of an average bunch. Southampton are in a similar position, relatively rookie manager Stuart Gray having his work cut out with an ageing Matt Le Tissier but a promising strike force of Marian Pahars and James Beattie to work with. Glen Hoddle had moved from Southampton to Tottenham in April 2001 and his squad at White Hart Lane was laced with experience – Les Ferdinand, Teddy Sheringham, Tim Sherwood, Darren Anderton and Gustavo Poyet all have plenty to offer, but in defence only a 20 year old Ledley King stands out. That could be a problem.

West Ham had finished 15th the previous season but with Harry Redknapp replaced by Glenn Roeder and young talent breaking through such as Joe Cole, Michael Carrick and Jermain Defoe, there was plenty of reason for optimism at Upton Park. The sometimes sublime and often ridiculous Paolo Di Canio was also a key figure, along with Fredi Kanoute and Trevor Sinclair. Also looking to break out of the middle of the pack are Middlesbrough, who had "won" the race to appoint long-time Fergie assistant Steve McClaren as manager. We all know Steve went on to manage England (badly) but he did deliver a trophy in his time at Middlesbrough, but mid-table is probably as good as he can hope for this season. He does have current-day England manager Gareth Southgate at the back and Paul Ince in midfield, but he also has Phil Stamp and Joseph-DesireJob, so it's not all good news. Everton are a particular pickle, with

Walter Smith at the helm but a finance status of "insecure." David Moyes would be appointed towards the end of the season but let's see how long Walter lasts here. He's brought Gazza to Goodison, but he's 34. I probably wouldn't let him share a room with Duncan Ferguson on away trips. They also have a 15 year old Wayne Rooney, who is barely rated and has the wrong date of birth. Little did they know…

That leaves us with the real life relegation trio. Ipswich Town are rated pretty highly by the game, having just finished fifth under the guidance of George Burley. Other than Finidi George, their squad has little to shout about. Unless you want to shout about a very young Titus Bramble and Darren Bent. Whilst I don't think many predicted their fall from 5th to 18th, I would be shocked if they finished in the top 8. Derby County on the other hand have taken the gamble of bringing veteran Italian striker Fabrizio Ravanelli back to the Premier League. They already have Georgi Kinkladze so had this been 97/98 they'd be loving life. But it isn't, so they won't. That brings us to Leicester City, who had a season to forget. With it being the final season at Filbert Street, it's fair to say they were hoping for more than a 20th placed finish, but somehow appointing Dave Bassett in October didn't help. Bassett replaced Peter Taylor, who went from managing England for a game (and giving Beckham the captaincy) to being sacked by Leicester in under 12 months. They had Dennis Wise and Robbie Savage in the same team, so you can imagine the sympathy they got in relegation. They might not be as bad here though, as fortunately for Ade Akinbiyi 'clumsiness' isn't a rated skill.

As with the previous book I'll be keeping an eye on Scotland and Spain too. Celtic are the reigning Scottish Champions, with Larrson, Sutton, Hartson, Moravcik, Petrov and…Steve Guppy to call upon it is hardly surprising. Mind you, Rangers have Ronald De Boer, Tore Andre Flo, Barry Ferguson and Lorenzo Amoruso, so it should be a good battle. The Spanish League is much more than a two horse race. Real Madrid are the defending champions and have recruited Zinedine Zidane to help Steve McManaman out, so it's going to take something remarkable to stop them. In reality, that something remarkable was Rafa Benitez and Valencia, who won the title by 7 points from Deportivo. Barcelona struggled to 4th as the Catalans went through a rather strange period in their history under the management of Charly Rexach. I've loaded the Italian League as a "background league" which means I can see the results but I can't manage there. I don't want to, but it's nice to have the option.

2001/02 is a World Cup season, so I'm sure you can see where this is going. In January 2001, Sven-Goran Eriksson became the first foreign manager to take charge of the England national team, but here we are just 6 months later, replacing him with me. For you see, this really was a golden generation of English football, and all we have to show for it are a few quarter final appearances. After a terrible start to the qualifying campaign, Kevin Keegan resigned and Sven rode in to save the day. He's won 3 on the bounce, so my appointment will be hugely popular. Anyway, England sit 6 points behind Germany with a game in hand, and my first game in charge will be away in Germany at the start of September. We all know how that ended, so it's a pretty stupid move to try and live up to that. There have been songs written about Sven – and I won't rest until the same happens to me. I'm already considering Gazza for a recall.

There we go then, you're up to speed in a little over 2000 words. Hopefully you are fully immersed in 2001 and we can see what the game has in store. Shall we?

July

When you start multiple leagues on CM01/02 you get given a choice of when you want the game to start. In this case they are all European league so it doesn't really matter, they are within days or at least weeks of each other, but had I selected the Brazilian League for example I could start in February 2002 and the game will simulate the other league up to that point. That's actually quite fun if you want a short term challenge of say, trying to keep the bottom side in the Premier League up. In fact you can read some of my attempts at doing just that over on *The Higher Tempo Pres.* With that plug safely banked, let's see what everyone is up to.

Brazil win the Copa America, beating Chile 1-0 in the final. Juninho Pernambuca scored the winner, probably best known as the Juninho who was really good at free kicks for Lyon, rather than the Middlesbrough favourite. The tournament was held in Colombia and Argentina didn't take part citing security concerns, basically there was a big back and forth before the tournament (in real life I hasten to add, fortunately the game hasn't incorporated political matters at this time) which resulted in the tournament being cancelled, then reinstated, teams such as Argentina dropping out and the end result was Colombia winning on their own patch. Therefore it is with great relief that the in game version of the tournament passes by with minimal incident.

You can probably guess by that South American tangent that there isn't an awful lot happening on the transfer front. It is July 30th before a Premier League club really splashes some serious money, with Sunderland purchasing David Prutton from Nottingham Forest for £7.25m. That sounds a lot and it probably is, but before Prutton was an omnipresent TV pundit, he was a very promising and versatile player. He's only 19 so Peter Reid obviously thinks he can get value out of him for years to come. Prutton's actual playing career probably peaked with playing Premier League football at Southampton, but also during his time there he received a 10 match ban for pushing a referee having been red carded. Swings and roundabouts.

Away from the transfer market, some Premier League clubs have been in competitive action thanks to the Intertoto cup. For those not familiar, the now-defunct Intertoto Cup was a backdoor into European competition for teams who really wanted to be in Europe but weren't good enough. In 2001/02, three teams could qualify for the UEFA Cup by going through multiple rounds of low quality action against other teams who also didn't qualify by natural means. This was later increased to 11 teams in 2006, which is really ludicrous when you think about it. Anyway, England had two entrants in the summer of 2001: Aston Villa and

Newcastle United. Both exited at the first round stage, Villa losing out to AIK of Sweden despite a late goal from Alpay, whilst Newcastle were humbled 3-0 away to Pribram of the Czech Republic. It's a tough place to go.

The Scottish Premier League gets underway on July 28th. That seems early. Celtic aren't bothered, they win 4-0 against St. Johnstone with two goals for John Hartson and one each for Henrik Larrson and Didier Agathe. All within the first half an hour. Rangers grind out a 1-0 win at Dundee United thanks to Barry Ferguson.

There is nothing else of note to tell you, it's really been a quiet start.

August

The FA are pleased with my performance. I have literally just sat here, I haven't even been into my office yet. Maybe they just gave me Sven's performance review to save them writing a new one? Don't worry, I'll soon turn that 'pleased' around.

Ipswich are the next team to open the chequebook. They've spent £3.4m on the flamboyant Jay-Jay Okocha. Okocha is somewhat strangely labelled as a defensive midfielder on the game, I'm sure anybody who saw this man play would consider it brave to have him shield the back four, but who am I to argue? Okocha would actually come to the Premier League in 2002, joining Bolton, where he brought his unique brand of skills to the Reebok which saw kids up and down the country trying to copy what I believe is now termed a 'rainbow flick'. One thing the game does have right is that his flair stat is 20, it'll be interesting to see how he does at Portman Road.

It's Liverpool's turn to be in competitive action, taking the tough trip to Israel to face Maccabi Haifa, who have a young Yossi Benayoun in their ranks. Liverpool win 1-0 thanks to Emile Heskey – Michael Owen is out for two weeks with a hamstring injury, which will most likely be a theme.

That warms Liverpool up for the Charity Shield, where they face Manchester United. Perhaps feeling the effects of the long trip in midweek, Liverpool rest a few including Robbie Fowler and Steven Gerrard but still manage to pull the score back to 2-2 having been 2-0 down to goals from Yorke and Veron. Liverpool's two goals come from Igor Biscan, which is pretty inexplicable. Andy Cole climbs off the bench to score the winner as Man Utd win 3-2 and take the first silverware of the season. It's a pretty entertaining season opener and hopefully a sign of things to come.

A news item drops into my list that all clubs are desperate to renew player contracts due to a change in transfer rules. This proposed reform will mean that players are only bound to a contract for 3 years (under 28) or 2 years (over 28). So, basically, if you have a 25 year old player who signed a contract 2 years and 6 months ago, in 6 months' time they can be offered a contract by another club, which if they accept, you will be given compensation for that player and he will move during the designated International transfer windows. This later came to be known as "The Webster Ruling" after Hearts defender Andy Webster invoked it in 2006. It is a legal minefield and the discussion over compensation amounts rumbled on for a couple of years. It's a move that gives bargaining power to the player but it is rarely straightforward, and something we'll not have to deal with here.

The first day of the Premier League is here! The most high profile clash sees Leeds welcome Liverpool to Elland Road, with Liverpool taking a 2-0 win thanks to Robbie Fowler and that man Igor Biscan, making an early dash for Player of the Year. Fowler does manage to break a toe shortly after scoring which makes him a big doubt for my upcoming clash with Germany, and with Owen still

10 days away from recovery, it is not welcome news. Defending Champions Manchester United ease to a 2-0 win over Blackburn with goals from Veron and Yorke, who are already looking like a devastating combination. Arsenal labour to a 1-0 win over Newcastle thanks to Kanu, whilst Derby's 2-0 win at Leicester is enough to give them top spot. It's a quiet opening to the season, with only 9 games as Chelsea and Charlton don't play for no apparent reason.

The Scottish League is now 4 games old, and we have new leaders! Dundee stun Celtic with a 2-1 win, their goalkeeper Jamie Langfield gets a perfect 10 rating in the process and Celtic drop to third. Rangers are second, only on goal difference, after Claudio Reyna leads them to a 1-0 win at home to Hearts. The goals aren't exactly flowing at Ibrox but it is early days yet. The Spanish league gets underway tomorrow.

I'm invited to name my squad for the games with Germany and Albania. Fowler and Owen are both doubtful, but I can't go without them. Andy Cole can't get in the Man Utd team which leaves Heskey as the only striker in the squad with games under his belt. That's not a situation any manager should have to deal with. The alternatives are not exactly awe inspiring. Young Alan Smith at Leeds is just recovering from injury, he hasn't played yet this season. There's Matt Jansen at Blackburn, but he's uncapped. I scroll through the list of names and hover my finger over the 'Resign' button. Michael Ricketts? Marcus Bent? Marcus Stewart? Jason Euell? All awful options. In fact, Euell went on to declare for Jamaica in real life after deciding that England call was never going to come. In Sven's time of need, he turned to Darius Vassell. Good old Darius can't get in the Villa team though, he's behind Dion Dublin in the pecking order. Dion Dublin you say? An obvious choice.

I don't know what they are doing at Leeds but Rio Ferdinand is out for a month. I could have done with him. In Ant & Dec's *We're on the Ball* he's an integral part of the song. Campbell to Rio, Rio to Scholesy, and so on. My options to replace him are Martin Keown, Gareth Southgate or a very young Jonathan Woodgate. I'll add Wes Brown to the mix, that'll help. I've resisted the temptation to bring Gazza, but I can't rule it out long term.

The Spanish League gets underway on Sunday 19th August, again it's a bit of a punctured fixture list with Real Madrid not in action. Barcelona win 2-1 at Malaga having been 2-0 up inside 5 minutes thanks to Kluivert and Saviola. Valencia though suffer a 2-1 loss at Sevilla.

Whoever came up with the scheduling on this game obviously didn't have my continuous narrative in mind. There's a full program of midweek games, the pick of which is Arsenal travelling to Chelsea, who are getting their season underway. Arsenal lead through a Patrick Vieira goal but it is cancelled out by Mikael Forssell, and the spoils are shared. Man Utd move into top spot with a 2-0 win at Derby, whilst Leeds are bottom after a 2-1 loss at Newcastle. 18 year old Jermaine Defoe scores twice as West Ham beat Middlesbrough 3-0 to take an early 2nd place. It's all meaningless right now of course. Having a browse of West Ham's squad, Glenn Roeder has rather boldly opted to list Fredi Kanoute for loan, despite him being one of the three star players. There are no games in Scotland or Spain, but there are Champions League qualifiers second legs. Liverpool win 4-0, with 2 goals for Heskey and who else but Igor Biscan, and Michael Owen was back on the bench. That is music to my ears with the Germany game 10 days away. I'm not sure how I missed this before, but Celtic and Rangers have drawn each other in these playoffs.
That...shouldn't be possible. Celtic won 1-0 at Celtic Park and thanks to a Henrik Larsson hat-trick, they secure a 3-3 draw at Ibrox and qualify for the group stages. Don't go out in Glasgow that night. The big shock of the night sees Barcelona lose on penalties to FC Copenhagen. To the

surprise of nobody, it is three Dutch players who fluff their lines – Overmars, Kluivert and Cocu the guilty parties as the Danish side advance to the group stages.

It's soon Saturday again and the last action before the International break. Please, nobody get injured. Unless you're German, in which case go nuts. I need all the help I can get. Juan Veron takes his tally to 4 in 4 as Man Utd hammer Southampton 4-0. Arsenal are up into second after Vieira and Henry see off Charlton. Leeds are off the bottom after a 2-0 win over Chelsea, who have Emmanuel Petit sent off for a two footed lunge on Lee Bowyer. At this time, everybody hates Lee, so it's not really a surprise. He does score Leeds' second though, so I doubt he cares. Teddy Sheringham scores twice as Tottenhan win 4-1 at Fulham. Maybe I should consider Teddy? Meanwhile at Portman Road, Sheringham's ex-strike partner Alan Shearer is dismissed for two yellow cards as Newcastle draw 1-1 at Ipswich. Jay-Jay Okocha rams in Ipswich's equaliser for his first goal in English football.

North of the border, Rangers are the new leaders after winning 4-0 at Dunfermline. They overhaul Dundee's goal difference despite The Dees beating Aberdeen 2-1. Celtic are a point behind after a 4-0 thrashing of Livingson. La Liga continues to confuse me, as Real Madrid sit out another match day. Turns out they have the Super Copa against Zaragoza and they played that over the first two weekends, with Zaragoza the unlikely winners. Barcelona draw 1-1 at home to Deportivo, Saviola snatching a late equaliser and relieving some of the early pressure on Rexach.

Mark Kerr is one of the so called wonderkids on this game who never quite hit the heights in real life. He's got a move to Rangers from Falkirk here for £1m, so hopefully he'll go on to great things. I met Kerr recently at *The FM17 Project* event in Glasgow and he was a great sport about the whole thing, as I've read stories about other players being somewhat bitter that they didn't live up to their Championship Manager potential. Kerr is back at Falkirk in real life and is the club captain.

September

The first day of September is the most important day in September. Germany vs England. We really have to win to stand a chance of going through automatically. It doesn't have to be 5-1 either. Any win will do.

Germany vs England – As it happened

There are some rivalries that just keep cropping

up. Fortunately, this occasion can't go to penalties. It's a 2002 World Cup qualifier, where Germany know if they can avoid defeat they will have one foot in the finals, and England will have to make do with a playoff spot. When the teams met in the last game at the old Wembley 11 months ago, Germany won 1-0 through a Dietmar Hamann free kick. That was the end for Kevin Keegan, who resigned just hours later, and brought us the joy of Sven, who won three on the bounce to make things look respectable. But now Sven's out and I am in, and with my much loved 4-3-1-2, I'm going to try and follow in his footsteps here in Berlin (not Munich, as in real life), where the attendance is expected to be over 75,000.

With that, let's look at the team news. Michael Owen has made it, which I am extremely relieved about it. He and Heskey lead the line, with Paul Scholes just behind them. I am torn between the experience of Steve McManaman and the youthful exuberance of Joe Cole, I've opted for the latter because Macca isn't anywhere near the Real Madrid team. Jonathan Woodgate will partner Sol Campbell and although Gary Neville is struggling with a bruised shin, I really don't want to have to play Danny Mills here, so it's a risk I'm willing to take. Richard Wright is in goal, he is ahead of Seaman for Arsenal and if he's good enough for Wenger, he's good enough for me. Germany have opted for 3-4-1-2, with wingbacks and Mehmet Scholl having a license to get forward. It's going to be difficult.

Germany: Kahn, Linke, Nowotny, Heinrich, Frings, Bode, Deisler, Ballack, Scholl, Neuville, Jancker
Subs: Baumann, Rost, Klose, Rehmer, Hamann, Bobic, Asamoah

England: R Wright, G Neville, Campbell, Woodgate, Ash. Cole, J. Cole, Gerrard, Beckham, Scholes, Heskey, Owen. **Subs:** Seaman, Brown, Bridge, Barmby, McManaman, Lampard, An. Cole
Let's get this over with.

KICK OFF – Germany get us underway here in the Olympiastadion.

2 mins – Positive start from England, passing the ball around well. Paul Scholes finds Steven Gerrard who tries his luck from the edge of the box, but it's a couple of yards over.

5 mins – England force a couple of corners, which Beckham delivers with his usual curve and dip but the German defence hold firm.

10 mins – For a small-ish player, Michael Owen doesn't half get a lot of headed chances. Gary Neville delivers the cross and Owen's movement

sees him get free in the box. His header is low to Oliver Kahn's right but the big stopper is down to parry the ball out, and Thomas Linke completes the clearance.

16 mins – More England pressure. Jonathan Woodgate hoists one forward and Owen out paces his man to latch on to the bouncing ball. The Liverpool man takes the shot early from the angle of the box but it goes over the bar. It'll come!

21 mins – Joe Cole, earning just his second England cap, is having a great time out there. He picks the ball up on the half way line and drives towards the German box. The German defence retreats and Cole fires in a shot from the edge of the box and that goes inches wide. What a run, a great effort from the West Ham man.

28 mins – The game has got a bit scrappy and nothing sums that up more than this tussle between Ballack and Gary Neville. The referee deems that Neville has fouled Ballack, and Germany have a free kick right on the edge of the box.

29 mins – **GOAL FOR GERMANY! Germany 1 – 0 England (Mehmet Scholl)**

Is there a German expression for sucker punch? England have been brilliant in the opening half an hour but this is brilliant from Mehmet Scholl. The Bayern Munich man sets his sights, lifts his free kick up and over the wall and leaves Richard Wright helpless as it settles in the top corner of his goal. The stadium is rocking, and England have it all to do.

32 mins – England look to respond but Kahn is out well at the feet of Joe Cole as he looks to latch onto a loose ball.

34 mins – Ashley Cole! What are you doing? Cole picks up the ball in his own half and runs down the left. He's invited to keep running, before getting a nosebleed 25 yards from goal and letting fly with his left foot which nearly catches out Kahn but he turns it behind for a corner.

35 mins – The corner is a bit of a scramble, Woodgate knocking it down to Scholes who can't quite get his shot away and Germany scramble it clear.

39 mins – England have a freekick wide on the left after Scholl fouls Scholes. It's another dangerous delivery from Beckham but Ballack heads it away. England running out of time to respond before half

time.

42 mins – **YELLOW CARD**

Ashley Cole clatters Carsen Jancker out on the touchline and referee Tarmo Sirel brandishes a yellow card.

45 mins – There will be two added minutes.

45+2 mins – Germany threaten a second, Oliver Neuville goes on a run and outstrips Sol Campbell. He bends a shot towards goal but it is too high. That'll be it for the first half.

HALF TIME: Germany 1 – 0 England

England have had the better of the chances and possession but Germany have the better of the all-important stat with that Mehmet Scholl free kick. It's not beyond England to come back but Germany are one of the last teams you'd want to be behind against.

KICK OFF – England get the game restarted, needing to overturn this deficit to keep any automatic qualification hopes alive.

48 mins – Another save! Emile Heskey gets on the end of a Beckham cross and he diverts the ball

towards the bottom corner with an outstretched left boot. It might beat some goalkeepers but Oliver Kahn is once again equal to it, at the cost of yet another corner.

49 mins – Set pieces might be a way back into this for England. Although Beckham's initial delivery is cleared, Joe Cole picks up the loose ball and drill in a low cross. Scholes controls, spins his man and hits a low shot and guess what? Kahn saves. It's good handling and it needed to be as the penalty area was full of English players hoping for a tap in.

54 mins – Germany have a free kick wide on the right which Sebastian Deisler delivers. Jancker wins the flick on and Scholl rolls it across the box where Thomas Linke's eyes are widening ready for a tap in. Sol Campbell has other ideas though and hooks it away in the nick of time. A bit of a let off for England.

58 mins – England will be thinking of a change soon. How many minutes does Michael Owen have in his legs? Fortunately Gary Neville's bruised shin doesn't seem to be much of an issue.

61 mins – Speaking of Gary Neville, here he is getting forward down the right. He beats Bode with the old knock and run and puts in a dangerous cross on the run. Steven Gerrard arrives

on the scene but his header goes over the bar. Keep trying, lads.

64 mins – Oh for goodness sake. An England attack breaks down as Neville's cross towards Heskey is gathered by Kahn. That's not much of a surprise, but what's this? Michael Owen is down, and he needs to come off. This is literally the opposite of the script.

65 mins – **England Substitution**

Andy Cole (he'll never be Andrew to me) is on for the stricken Owen. Now what for England?

70 mins – We now have three Cole's on the pitch for England, which might get confusing. I'll refer to them by first name. Andy is loitering in the box but Heinrich intercepts at the cost of a corner.

71 mins – **GOAL FOR ENGLAND! Germany 1 – 1 England (Jonathan Woodgate)**

Finally! Another Beckham corner and this time Jonathan Woodgate leaps like a salmon above Thomas Linke and powers his header in off the underside of the bar. It's only his second cap. The England bench breathe a sigh of relief, but a draw won't really help.

72 mins – England are rampant now. Gerrard plays a ball 40 yards over the top and Andy Cole controls it brilliantly. He hits a low right footed shot across Kahn, for once the veteran stopper can't get near it but the post denies England. This is breathless stuff

73 mins – **GOAL FOR ENGLAND! Germany 1 – 2 England (Joe Cole)**

All the Cole's! It starts with Gary Neville and Steven Gerrard working the ball out of a tight corner, before Gerrard finds Andy Cole. Andy lays it off to Ashley, who goes galloping down the left again and his cross misses everyone, except the arriving Joe Cole, who shows the composure of a seasoned International by controlling the ball before steering a right footed shot beyond Kahn. England lead!

74 mins – **Germany Substitution.** I imagine this was planned before the goal as it is like for like, with Carsten Jancker coming off to be replaced by Fredi Bobic.

77 mins – This Cole triangle is probably the key to us not only qualifying but winning the World Cup. Joe and Ashley combine again, Ashley's shot is travelling but Kahn parries it away and Deisler clears.

79 mins – **Substitution for Germany.**

Two in fact. Hamann is on for Deisler, and Frank Baumann replaces Thomas Linke. I'm not sure that will help.

81 mins – England are going for the kill. Manchester United team mates Andy Cole and Beckham combine, Beckham curls an effort towards the far post and Kahn makes yet another save.

82 mins – **YELLOW CARD**

Andy Cole is chasing back following that Kahn save and he trips Michael Ballack, somewhat cynically. It's an obvious yellow.

84 mins – **Substitution for England.** Second England change, with Frank Lampard replacing Paul Scholes.

85 mins – **DISALLOWED GOAL.** Somebody pick my stomach up off the floor please. Scholl delivers a free kick into the area, which Emile Heskey defends manfully. Heinrich picks up the loose ball and sends it back to Scholl, who curls in a delicious cross and Frank Baumann, the substitute, heads in the equaliser. The stadium erupts but the linesman has his flag up. Fredi Bobic was offside. Thank you

Fredi.

88 mins – Gerrard, Lampard and Joe Cole are keeping the ball, trying to run the clock down. Joe spots an opportunity though and heads for the box, before a curling a shot well over the bar. Go to the corner man!

90 mins – Three added minutes. Don't you dare!

90+2 mins – Chance! Hamann finds Neuville, who makes space on the far side of the box but his shot is well over the bar. All power and no accuracy. England are nearly there.

FULL TIME: Germany 1 – 2 England

England got there in the end. Germany managed 3 shots all game, with the one that went in being their only effort on target. By contrast England hit the target 8 times from their 15 efforts. England dominated this game and it would have been an injustice if they had lost it.

Owen is out for three weeks. I'm so happy, Gazza is called up as his replacement. We play Albania up in Newcastle (Wembley is being renovated) and it'll be a sentimental moment, especially as Andy Cole will probably start up front. We could do with winning by at least three to ahead of Germany on goal difference, which remains an obstacle.

Elsewhere, Ireland stuffed Holland 4-1 to secure at least a playoff spot. Scotland defeat Croatia 2-0 to give themselves a fighting chance of qualification, whilst Italy and Spain are already there. Sadly Northern Ireland and Wales are already eliminated.

With it being the International break, there is nothing to report on the intervening days. We're off to Newcastle for the Albania clash, where goals are the order of the day. Andy Cole will replace Michael Owen, whilst Ashley Cole is one yellow away from a ban but I'll play him anyway. We can't take any chances.

England vs Albania – As it happened

Mick Lowes, a former BBC Radio Newcastle commentator, would call any match after a big win "after the Lord Mayor's show." I have no idea where that saying originates from, but I am sure it applies in cases like this. The England roadshow has arrived at St James' Park, Newcastle for a clash with Albania. Albania are the bottom team in group 9, with just one win, against Greece way back at the start of the campaign. A win for

England and they will go to 16 points, joint top with Germany and then it'll be all about goal difference going into the final game. We'll worry about that later. Let's see the team news.

Andy Cole starts on a ground where he scored so many goals earlier in his career. Granted, he is not well liked for his departure to Man Utd, but I'm hoping he'll ignore all that and score a hatful. Robbie Fowler is about 80% fit, so he can be a sub. I've put Gascoigne on the bench. Don't judge me. Albania have a flat back 5 and I'm afraid I don't know any of their players.

England: Wright, G Neville, Ash. Cole, Woodgate, Campbell, Gerrard, Beckham, J Cole, Scholes, An. Cole, Heskey. **Subs:** Seaman, Brown, Bridge, Lampard, Gascoigne, Dublin, Fowler.

Albania: Strakosia, Zoumba, Bashi, Fakaj, Cipi, Murati, Chatzi, Hasi, Lala, Vata, Tare. **Subs:** Bozgo, Beqaj, Deliuh, Toku, Bledar, Kuci, Bushaj.

An early goal would be nice. I don't want to let down the Geordie public.

KICK OFF – England get us underway, and immediately Albania drop in to what is pretty much a back 9.

2 mins – England are perhaps a little bit complacent here, giving the ball away and Gary Neville is lucky to escape a yellow card for pulling back Edwin Murati. Murati is at Lille and has a 20 rating for crossing, so maybe Gary was right to foul him. The free kick comes to nothing.

4 mins – Andy Cole has a go from fully 30 yards and is nowhere near. Stick to being in the penalty area, Andy.

5 mins – It's one way traffic. Cole cushions a header into the path of Emile Heskey, who fires his shot straight at Strakosia who gathers it relatively easily. You'd want that combination to be the other way round, really.

8 mins – **YELLOW CARD**

Ashley Cole has become a key attacking outlet and he gets away down the left before being pulled back by Ervin Fakaj. It's a yellow card without doubt.

11 mins – Heskey has a headed chance this time, but he can't connect properly with Andy Cole's cross and it goes well wide.

13 mins – Beckham spins a free kick into the box, Steven Gerrard flicks on but Strakosia punches the

ball away under pressure. Surely a goal is imminent for England?

17 mins – Woodwork! England are so dominant it isn't even a surprise that Gary Neville latches on to a Joe Cole pass. He is denied by a great last ditch tackle but the ball falls loose for David Beckham who takes aim with a first time shot than crashes off the cross bar. The ball falls for Paul Scholes who steadies himself and sends the ball back towards goal, only for Strakosia to turn it behind for a corner.

18 mins – Remember England's equaliser in Germany 4 days ago? Beckham's corner is headed at goal by Jonathan Woodgate, but it goes a yard or so wide.

20 mins – Paul Scholes is the latest to try and gift Emile Heskey a goal, chipping the ball into the box perfectly for big Emile to direct a header goalwards but that man Strakosia tips it wide. If there is ever a break in play, I will tell you who he is.

21 mins – The corner is rubbish. Let's research

25 mins – Fotis Strakosia is 36 and plays for Ionikos, a Greek club. He played for Olympiakos earlier in the 90s. He is a nuisance.

29 mins – There's been another flurry of corners but Beckham's radar is briefly broken and there's not a chance to report. Have Albania survived the storm?

33 mins – I don't know how England haven't scored. This time Beckham's corner is met powerfully by Woodgate, and Strakosia keeps it out at full stretch. It's cleared to Joe Cole on the edge of the box who smashes a low shot and guess what? Saved again. It's cleared. It's still 0-0.

37 mins – England would take any goal before half time.

41 mins – For England I mean! Albania have a corner and Tare gets above Ashley Cole but can only direct his header wide. Bit of a let off.

45 mins – 1 minute added on to end this half

HALF TIME: England 0 – 0 Albania

How? England need to win 3-0 to go top of the table but at some point the concern is going to be getting three points.

KICK OFF - Albania restart the game.
49 mins – England haven't started with the same fluency. The St. James' Park faithful are getting a

little bit restless.

53 mins – More England corners, more Albanian heads. I would say changes were the answer but some idiot named Gazza and Dion Dublin amongst the 7 subs.

58 mins – Actually nothing at all happening now. Concern is etched on England faces.

64 mins – **PENALTY TO ENGLAND**

Now, this is a chance. Paul Scholes rides one challenge and before he can shoot, Murati jumps in with a two footed lunge and gets nowhere near the ball. A stonewall penalty and he's lucky it's only a yellow card. But who will take it?

65 mins – **GOAL FOR ENGLAND! England 1 – 0 Albania (Ashley Cole)**

I confess, I had Owen set as the penalty taker with Fowler as second choice. With neither on the pitch, Ashley Cole grabs the ball and sends the keeper the wrong way. Finally, England lead!

68 mins – **Substitution for Albania**. Murati, having given a way the penalty and being booked, is replaced by Farat Toku, a 20 year old left sided

midfield player from Bochum.

72 mins – **Substitution for Albania.** Second change for Albania as Bushaj comes on for Vata.

74 mins - Emile Heskey might never score again. His latest effort is yet another header that is gathered by Strakosia.

75 mins – Joe Cole hasn't been as lively as he was in Berlin but he is the latest to be denied by Strakosia.

76 mins – **Substitution for England**. Off comes Emile Heskey, on comes Dion Dublin.

77 mins – Maybe that change was a mistake? Albania have a rare foray forwards and the newly arrived Bushaj shoots from just outside the box, but it's about a yard over the bar.

78 mins – **GOAL FOR ENGLAND! England 2 – 0 Albania (Paul Scholes)**

A goal made in Manchester. Gary Neville gets free down the right and from the byline, he pulls the ball back to Andy Cole on the edge of the box. Cole turns and lays the ball off for the arriving Paul Scholes who rifles a low shot beyond the practically unbeatable Strakosia. Relief all round.

79 mins – **GOAL FOR ENGLAND! England 3 – 0 Albania (Paul Scholes)**

Where has this been? Clinical from Scholes, Ashley Cole crosses from the left and Paul Scholes is standing unmarked on the penalty spot to slam home his second and England's 3rd. Gazza is ready...

80 mins – **Substitution for England.** Gerrard off, Paul Gascoigne on. St James' Park rises to applaud one of their favourite sons, whilst simultaneously shaking their heads.

84 mins – England are seeing the game out now. This will put them top of the table heading in to the final game at home to Greece, whilst Germany host Finland.

90 mins – There'll be three added minutes.

FULL TIME – England 3 – 0 Albania

England are top of the group, 21 shots later. There is work still to be done, but we'll head to Old Trafford in a month knowing that it is in our hands.

Scotland lose 2-0 in Belgium, but even though they are third, all is not lost. Croatia are only ahead of the Scots on goal difference, and both sit 3 points behind Belgium. Croatia host Belgium in the final game, so there's a chance that if Scotland win they can at least make the playoffs. However, Belgium's goal difference is much better than Scotland's, so not that much of a chance. We'll see. There's not an awful lot else to report, as we finally end International week.

Back to club action and Saturday 8th September sees Man Utd cement their place at the top of the league with a 5-0 thrashing of Everton. It's a ludicrous game where Everton have 3 men sent off and Man Utd are awarded two penalties, but the referee is Uriah Rennie so that explains that. Over at Elland Road, Leeds put 7 past Derby in a ruthless display. Kewell, Viduka, Bowyer, McPhail and Robbie Keane share the goals whilst Rio Ferdinand returns from injury, and Leeds are up to 6th. Arsenal remain 2nd with a 3-0 win over Southampton, who are kept off the bottom only by Bolton, who lose 1-0 at Newcastle. Tottenham are third after scoring four away from home for the second consecutive game, this time at Aston Villa. The Old Firm meet at Ibrox and Henrik Larsson saves Celtic with an 83rd minute equaliser, but Dundee can't take advantage as they lose 3-2 at Livingston. In Spain, Real Madrid finally play their first game of the season but they can only draw 1-1 at home to Celta. Luis Enrique scores a second half winner for Barcelona away at Valladolid to regain top spot.

The Champions League is back! This is during the slightly silly phase where the tournament had two group stages, so here we are on match day one of the first group stage. It's a good night for Liverpool, beating Panathinaikos 3-0 with Biscan once again amongst the scorers. They're in a group with Juventus, though the Italian giants lose 1-0 away to Sparta Prague. Manchester United are 2-0 victors over Boavista of Portugal, with Lazio also in the group. Celtic make it a trio of British wins as they edge FC Copenhagen 2-1. As with the modern day, the fixtures are split over Tuesday and Wednesday night, with the second night seeing Arsenal suffer a 1-0 loss away to Spartak Moscow. Sol Campbell misses a penalty. Should have let Ashley Cole take it. The UEFA Cup kicks off on Thursday, but I'm only going to bring you the second leg summaries.

Before we get on to the weekend, we have transfer news to catch up on. Blackburn have paid £825k to bring Graeme Le Saux back to Ewood Park, having gone back to Chelsea from Blackburn in 1997. Confused? Imagine how Graeme feels. Le Saux has 36 England caps but I doubt I'll be making it 37.

Ipswich meanwhile have shelled out £1m to bring Aaron Winter to Portman Road. Winter has 84 caps for Holland and had been at the successful Inter Milan team of the late 90s, before returning to Ajax in 1999. At 34, it's quite late for him to arrive in the Premier League but I'm sure he and Okocha will form a famous partnership. Thomas Helveg, the Danish full back, has signed for Fulham for £1.5m. Helveg had lost his place in the Milan team and at 30, he still has some good years ahead of him. In real life he went to Norwich during their relegation season 2004/05 and didn't pull up many trees.

Back to the action now and Man Utd win *again*, that's 7 in a row in all competitions. Andy Cole nabbed the winner in a 1-0 win away at Sunderland. Liverpool have had a very average start and that continues with a 1-0 defeat at home to Newcastle. Gary Speed (RIP) with the only goal there. It's double delight in the North East as Middlesbrough earn a 2-1 win at Spurs, Paul Ince playing the perfect 10 rating and getting the winner. That puts the North East pair 4th and 3rd respectively. Southampton score their first goals of the campaign and get their first win in the process, defeating Leeds 2-1 at St Mary's. That means Bolton are back to the bottom, suffering a cruel 90th minute defeat against Chelsea at The Reebok. Former Trotter Eidur Gudjohnsen scored the crucial goal to rub salt into open Lancastrian wounds. In Scotland, Rangers are hammered 5-2 at Pittodrie, but Celtic ease to a 3-1 win against Kilmarnock. Meanwhile in Spain, Real Madrid find themselves in the relegation zone after a 2-1 defeat against Real Betis. Barcelona win 2-0 against Alaves but Real Sociedad go top after a 4-0 success against Espanyol. Of course, Real Madrid have two games in hand on most of the table so I'm sure they won't be panicking yet.

The Champions League games come thick and fast it seems, as we're back in European mode for a second consecutive midweek. What's Spanish for panic? Real Madrid lose 2-1 away to Borussia Dortmund, and coupled with their draw at home to Nantes in the first set of matches, the table makes sorry reading after 2 games. It makes rather better reading for Arsenal, who defeat Parma 2-0 thanks to a Thierry Henry double. The Wednesday games are a bleak night for English football. The unbeatable Man Utd are humbled 3-0 by Lazio in Rome, whilst Liverpool suffer a 1-0 reverse against Juventus in Turin. Give a big hand to Celtic though – they win 2-0 away at Bayern Munich thanks to a Tommy Boyd double. Who else? There's also some 2nd round League Cup ties, as Division 3 Luton grab the headlines by defeat high-flying Middlesbrough 2-0 at Kenilworth Road. West Ham are also in the news for the wrong reasons, losing in extra time to

Port Vale. At least Robbie Williams will be happy.

1-0 to the Arsenal! The Gunners edge Bolton thanks to an early Robert Pires goal which rounds off a good week for Wenger's men. Man Utd brush off their European defeat by making it 6 league wins out of 6, defeating Fulham 1-0 thanks to Ruud Van Nistelrooy's second half goal. Chelsea and Liverpool grind out a 1-1 draw, a result which satisfies nobody except Emile Heskey who finally gets his first league goal of the season. A Mark Viduka double sees Leeds win 2-0 against West Ham, lifting the Whites up to 6th, whilst Newcastle's home defeat to Charlton allows Ipswich to jump into 4th, Aaron Winter netting a debut goal in their home win against Southampton. Middlesbrough retain 3rd with a comfortable 2-0 win over Blackburn and Spurs round off the top 5 after a hard fought 2-2 draw at Leicester. Celtic and Rangers both won, meaning Celtic remain two points clear after 8 games, whilst the panic is over in Spain as Real Madrid thrash Las Palmas 4-1. Barcelona lose 1-0 in Bilbao, meaning Real Sociedad retain top spot despite their 2-1 loss to a Martin Palermo inspired Villarreal.

It's time to name my England squad for the Greece game. It's a squad of many changes now that the players have played more than one competitive fixture for their clubs, I can actually judge who is in form. For example, Danny Mills has been loaned to Rotherham. So he's out. Phil Neville has played every game for Man Utd, in he comes. Gazza and Dublin are regretfully cut, but Bowyer and Sheringham have been in great form for their clubs so are their replacements. Rio Ferdinand is back from injury to replace Martin Keown, and finally Darren Anderton is in for Nicky Butt. We'll have a great time.

THREE consecutive weeks of Champions League football?! Real Madrid thrash Tirol Innsbruck of Austria 5-1, even Geremi gets on the scoresheet. Arsenal look set to win 1-0 in Lille but a 90th minute goal from Tony Vairelles snatches a point for the French side. Liverpool and Man Utd both return to winning ways with victories over Sparta Prague and Brann respectively. Andy Cole and Michael Owen were both amongst the goals which is good news for me. Celtic lose at home to PSV, as the football equilibrium returns to normal.

Those UEFA Cup second legs happened, too. Leeds were the most convincing winners, a 6-1 aggregate win against FC Brasov of Romania seeing them into round 2. Jonny Woodgate has sprained an ankle though. I know, what a shock. He's withdrawn from the squad and I call in Gareth Barry, who is a centre half or left back on the game despite playing on the left wing for England in

Euro 2000. Some things I can't explain. Jay-Jay Okocha helps Ipswich see off Polish side Pogon, Rangers secure a pair of 1-0 wins against Turkey's Gaziantepspor and Barcelona take out all their anger on Maccabi Tel-Aviv, winning 6-1 in Israel. It's been awful start for Chelsea though, drawing 0-0 against Dinamo Bucharest to exit the competition on away goals.

Another Saturday, another win for Alex Ferguson. Their 3-1 win at Charlton gives them 21 points from a possible 21, but Arsenal are 5 points behind with a game in hand after they won 2-1 at Derby. Dennis Bergkamp scored both goals. Ipswich climb to third after an entertaining 5-3 win at White Hart Lane. Spurs keeper Kasey Keller gets a 3 rating, which sounds generous. Mind you, Darren Anderton got a perfect 10 from right wing back for Spurs, so my decision to recall him looks a smart one. The Wear-Tees derby finishes 0-0, whilst Newcastle pile on the misery for West Ham with a 4-0 win at Upton Park. Bolton remain welded to the bottom, this time a 2-0 home reverse against Liverpool maintains their 100% losing record. Gerrard and Heskey got the goals, in more good England news. It's time for El Clasico in Spain, as Real Madrid take the spoils in the Nou Camp scoring with their only shot on target. Santiago Solari is the hero and Barcelona drop to 6th. Real Sociedad continue their strong start, beating

Malaga 2-0 to stay top, 1 point ahead of Real Betis. John Toshack is in charge of Real Sociedad, who is of course a former Real Madrid manager. The usual two results happened in Scotland...

One more transfer line to round off September, as Markus Babbel departs Liverpool for £9m. He's joined Borussia Dortmund, which will no doubt please former club Bayern Munich. Babbel was an integral part of Liverpool's successful 2000/01 season, and continued to be the first choice right back here, so his sale is a bit of a surprise. In real life during 2001/02, Babbel unfortunately contracted Guillain-Barre syndrome which put him out of action for over a year.

October

Amazingly, UEFA spare us a fourth consecutive week of action which allows the Premier League to have a full round of fixtures on the Wednesday evening. The big game comes at Anfield, where Arsenal are the visitors. A tight game is heading for a 0-0 draw until Patrick Berger is sent off on 86 minutes for raising his hands to Jermaine Pennant, who then scores an 89th minute winner. Pennant started ahead of Bergkamp, for reasons I can't really fathom. A solitary Ryan Giggs goal is enough for Man Utd to sneak a win at White Hart Lane and maintain their advantage, but Ipswich lose to a

Paolo Di Canio inspired West Ham to drop to 5th. Leeds are up to third, dishing up Bolton's 8th consecutive loss in the process whilst Sunderland are 4th after coming from behind to win at Charlton. Middlesbrough and Newcastle both lose, with Chelsea's 4-2 win at St James' Park particularly catching the eye. In Scotland, the third round of the Scottish League Cup saw Celtic & Rangers both advance, whilst Spain had a midweek off.

The schedulers at the FA have a lot of explaining to do. It would have been nice to have my players put their feet up 3 days before this vital qualifying clash but no, we had to have proper, competitive fixtures. I've lost Gerrard, Owen and Bowyer to injury. Consider me unamused.

The equation is simple – equal what Germany are doing, or better it. The good thing is the CM3 series introduced a "Latest Scores" tab during your game so you could see how your rivals are getting on. I thought it was amazing at the time. Anyway, let's go to Old Trafford and we'll try not to worry about how Germany are getting on against Finland.

England vs Greece – As it happened

It's the final round of European qualifying and Group 9 couldn't be tighter. England top the group with 16 points and a plus 8 goal difference, whilst Germany are second with the same points and a plus 7 goal difference. Germany have scored two more, so we have a tiny margin for error. Before I get on to the team news, this is of course the famous "Beckham free kick game" which by the way is ruined by Gary Bloom's commentary where he momentarily turns into Victor Meldrew. Look it up on YouTube, you'll see what I mean. Anyway, what I always find astonishing is that Germany drew 0-0 with Finland whilst we were messing about trailing twice to Greece. In many ways, that was the football miracle that day. That tangent aside, let's look at the teams.

England stick with the three Cole's and bring in Neville for Neville. That's Andy, Joe and Ashley and Phil for Gary, first name fans. Rio Ferdinand is back from injury to replace the stricken Woodgate, whilst Lampard replaces the injured Gerrard. Robbie Fowler joins Andy Cole up front with Heskey a substitute. Greece have Newcastle defender Nikos Dabizas at the heart of their 3 man defence as they opt for a 3-4-1-2, similar to the Germany formation last month.

England: Wright, P Neville, Ash. Cole, Ferdinand, Campbell, Lampard, Scholes, Beckham, J Cole, Fowler, An. Cole. **Subs:** Seaman, G Neville, Bridge,

Anderton, McManaman, Sheringham, Heskey.

Greece: Atmatzidis, Kopitsis, Grammozis, Vlachos, Dabizas, Patsatzoglou, Lakis, Tsartas, Vryzas, Nalitzis, Vilanakis. **Subs:** Vakuftsis, Eleftheropoulos, Borbokis, Georgatos, Nikolaidis, Amanatidis, Alexandris.

With all the pleasantries out of the way, the teams are ready to kick off. I will take this moment to point out that Greece are managed by Otto Rehhagel, who is German...

KICK OFF – England get us underway at a vociferous Old Trafford

2 mins – Barely underway and already the pendulum has swung. **Germany 1 – 0 Finland** after Carsten Jancker drills home a very early goal. That doesn't really change much for England, they need to win first!

5 mins – Uh oh. **Germany 2 – 0 Finland**. Mehmet Scholl has scored another memorable free kick and now the pressure is really on England.

6 mins – There is a game at Old Trafford but nothing is happening. The crowd have quietened now the Germany score is filtering through and the nerves are growing.

10 mins – David Beckham is trying to make things happen for his team, but his cross is claimed by Amatzidis with Andy Cole waiting.

14 mins – We asked you to do us one thing, Finland. **Germany 3 – 0 Finland**. Not even 5 minutes are on the clock, but Marco Bode has made it 3-0. Still 0-0 at Old Trafford though.

18 mins – England have been flat and they almost pay for it, Tsartas sends over a free kick and Nalitzis meets it with a firm header which Richard Wright does well to palm away.

22 mins – Here we go, England finally showing signs of life. Joe Cole has barely had a touch so far but he goes on a bit of a mazy run here, reaching the edge of the box before striking a low shot that is straight at Amatzidis.

25 mins – **Germany 4 – 0 Finland**. Oliver Neuville converts a penalty. He wasn't going to miss was he? England need to match this, somehow.

29 mins – **GOAL FOR ENGLAND! England 1 – 0 Greece (Sol Campbell)**

That's better! England are on the board, Beckham's latest pin-point corner is headed in by Sol Campbell. A splendid time to get your first England goal.

34 mins – Phil Neville! His great mate Paul Scholes picks him out at the far post, but Phil is not used to seeing the whites of the goalkeeper's eyes and his shot is tame and easy for Amatzidis.

36 mins – Greece aren't going to go away lightly. Richard Wright shows why he is the number one, first saving a header from Patsatzoglou before sprawling across his goal to save the rebound from Vryzas.

39 mins – **GOAL FOR ENGLAND! England 2 – 0 Greece (Frank Lampard)**

Another first International goal at a crucial time! Beckham is at the heart of the move, picking out Fowler in the box who lays the ball off to Joe Cole. Cole bursts past his man and squares the ball for Lampard who can't miss. Come on!

41 mins – **GOAL FOR ENGLAND! England 3 – 0 Greece (Ashley Cole)**

Ashley Cole goal machine! England are rampant, backed by a frenzied crowd who are maybe starting to believe again. A simple goal this, with an odd scorer. Phil Neville crosses, Lampard heads down and Ashley Cole takes it on the volley from about 10 yards. It's a striker's finish, right in the corner. One more!

45 mins – There'll be three added minutes

45+1 mins – **Red Card** in Berlin. Thorsten Frings has been sent off for punching Janne Saarinen in the face. Germany will have to play out the second half a man light but they are four goals to the good.

45+2 mins – **GOAL DISALLOWED**

This is harsh. David Beckham scores, the stadium goes mad as they are still digesting the red card news from Germany, but a pesky linesman has his flag up. It seems Frank Lampard was standing in an offside position when the shot was struck and the linesman has ruled it offside. Tough call, but England can't lose heart over it.

HALF TIME: England 3 – 0 Greece

Germany top the table on goals scored as it stands. England heading for a playoff, they find themselves in the rather strange position of being 3-0 up and disappointed. England will have a problem if Greece score, which you wouldn't rule out.

KICK OFF – Greece get the game restarted.

47 mins – Early free kick to start the half right on the edge of the Greece box. Beckham steps up and...plants it into the wall.

51 mins – **Substitution for Greece.** Vasilis Lakis is off and Alexandros Alexandris is on.

54 mins – Greece are really having a go. I don't care for it. New man Alexandris must have Germany blood or family, as he skins Phil Neville and picks out Vilanakis with a cross, but he shows no composure and misses by a mile.

57 mins – **GOAL FOR GREECE! England 3 – 1 Greece (Vasilis Tsartas)**

That's an onion in the ointment. Moments after Wright denies Vilanakis, an England break is snuffed out and with the game resembling a basketball match, Greece find themselves 3 on 2. Vilanakis feeds Tsartas and with all the time in the world inside the box, hits a low right footed shot beyond Wright. England need two more.

60 mins – **GOAL FOR ENGLAND! England 4 – 1 Greece (David Beckham)**

As you were. And what a goal! This game is ridiculous, but there is not a more popular scorer than David Beckham. Scholes finds Lampard,

Lampard goes square to Beckham, who has the option of Phil Neville on the overlap on taking a strike on from 30 yards. Obviously, he picks the latter and it goes in off the bar. A beautiful sight. England still need a goal from either themselves or Finland though.

63 mins – England need to show composure here, there's still plenty of time.

67 mins – Penalty! No! The England bench are livid. Robbie Fowler goes past Patsatzoglou in the box who hauls down the Liverpool man. It looks blatant but referee Keith Glasgow says no. Yep, Keith Glasgow.

71 mins – Tsartas, who as it stands is breaking England hearts, curls in a dangerous looking free kick which Wright does well to claim. All the action is at the wrong end for England though.

75 mins – **Substitution for Greece**. Greece make a second change, Grigoris Georgatos of Inter Milan is on for Dimitrios Grammozis. It was somewhat of a surprise that Georgatos didn't start the game for Greece.

78 mins – **Substitution for England.** England roll the dice, with Teddy Sheringham on for Andy Cole.

81 mins – **Substitution for England**. Another change, Steve McManaman is on for Paul Scholes.

84 mins – Chance for Greece, another Tsartas set piece, this time a corner, which Alexandris gets his head to but he can't direct it.

87 mins – It's all Greece, I think England have blown themselves out. Vilanakis tries his luck but it goes well wide. Richard Wright hurries to get the ball back.

89 mins – Greece are keeping the ball. You aren't even playing for anything!

90 mins – Is CM01/02 clever enough to make Rehhagel's nationality an issue here? 2 minutes added on.

90+2 mins – It's Greece with all the play, Vryzas heads a chance straight at Richard Wright though. England running out of time and ideas.

FULL TIME: England 4 – 1 Greece

GERMANY QUALIFY FOR WORLD CUP 2002

I feel sick. I know we did all we could by winning all three games but you know, I'm sure some people will blame me for bringing on Gazza and

Dion Dublin for the final 10 minutes against Albania. We could have scored an extra goal there. I prefer to blame Peter Taylor for drawing 0-0 against Finland. Bloody Finland. They've given us the Moomins but Moomins won't qualify us for the World Cup. Instead it's the playoffs, which is at least over two legs. Maybe Michael Owen can grace us with his presence for those games?

Just one midweek fixture, as Chelsea finally play their game in hand. It's a total demolition as well, dismantling Charlton 4-0 at Stamford Bridge. Gianfranco Zola plays the perfect 10 in getting a goal and an assist and Ranieri's men are up to 7th.

On to the weekend then and it's 9 out of 9 for Manchester United. They do concede their second goal of the season (to Alan Wright, of all people) but they win 3-1 at Villa Park. Arsenal cling on to their coat tails with another 1-0 win, this time at home to Fulham. Massive news from the Reebok though – Bolton have a point! Henrik Pedersen's equaliser secures a 2-2 draw and breaks their duck. Leeds are up to third as Keane & Viduka see off Sunderland, whilst Newcastle are 4th as Alan Shearer sees off former club Blackburn. In Spain, Barcelona's woes continues with a 0-0 draw away to Real Betis. That leaves the Catalan side in 5th. Real Madrid put 5 past Mallorca, even Makelele scored. Villarreal are the surprise leaders after just 7 games. Scotland continues as you would expect – Celtic and Rangers both win and there is already a 7 point gap back to third place St Johnstone.

There's double English delight in Tuesday's Champions League games, Smicer and Barmby scoring the goals that see Liverpool defeat Sparta Prague whilst Man Utd win 1-0 in Brann thanks to Ruud van Nistelrooy. Celtic trail 2-0 away to PSV but Chris Sutton climbs off the bench to score two penalties in the last 10 minutes to steal a point. An Englishman who scores penalties? That could be useful. Wednesday sees a truly remarkable event – Francis Jeffers scores a Champions League goal. He helps Arsenal to defeat Lille 3-0, whilst some fellow called Zidane scores during Real Madrid's 3-0 defeat of Tirol Innsbruck.

Finally! Manchester United drop points, a disappointing 0-0 draw at home to Middlesbrough. With Veron and Giggs injured, they lack creativity and it's a fairly quiet afternoon for Mark Schwarzer. Arsenal come from behind to defeat bitter rivals Spurs at White Hart Lane, whilst Newcastle are up to 3rd thanks to an 89th minute winner from Alan Shearer at Pride Park. Michael Owen is back (again) and scores twice in Liverpool's 4-0 win at Southampton, and Leeds are up to fourth after a 3-1 win at Fulham, who have slid to 17th. Meanwhile, Barcelona's nightmare continues with a 1-1 home draw with Celta Vigo, whilst future Real Madrid manager Aitor Karanka scores the only goal as Real Madrid defeat Real Zaragoza. As usual, Celtic and Rangers both win.

We're up to the fifth game in the first group stage of the Champions League, and Arsenal secure their passage into group stage two with a win from behind against Spartack Moscow. Manchester United are also through, their 2-0 win in Portugal against Boavista means they will battle Lazio next time for the top spot in the group. Liverpool are in trouble though, blowing a 1-0 lead in Greece to lose to an 89th minute goal against Panathinaikos. It means the two sides are locked together on 9 points, along with Juventus, with the Italian giants due to visit Anfield in the next match day. Celtic lose 2-1 in Copenhagen, and their group is such a mess that any of the four teams can qualify going into the final set of matches. Celtic will host Bayern Munich in that one though, who are oddly bottom of the group as it stands. We'll catch up with the UEFA Cup when the second legs are played.

Leicester City double Manchester United's goals against column, but their two goals are in vain as the defending champions make it 10 out of 10 with a 3-2 win at Filbert Street. Arsenal ease to victory against Blackburn to keep the pressure on, whilst

Newcastle's good recent form continues with a 4-1 thrashing of sorry Southampton. Liverpool's revival is checked with a 1-1 home draw against West Ham. Leeds thrash Tottenham 4-0 to keep their place in the top 4, but Bolton return to losing ways and already 6 points from safety. Celtic and Rangers take things to another level as both win 4-0. Barcelona plumb new depths by losing 2-1 to Mallorca, a young Samuel Eto'o getting the winner. Real Madrid lose a feisty game at Rafa Benitez's Valencia and have two men sent off in a minute in the process. Morientes and Raul take turns at slapping Roberto Ayala in the 9th minute and both are dismissed. Although Steve McManaman briefly has them on terms, big John Carew scores before Ayala settles it late on. Valencia are 14th and not looking likely to win the Championship they won in real life, with Barcelona 12th and Real Madrid 8th, though the games played are uneven throughout the division. Villarreal remain top despite losing 2-0 to Celta. A total mess.

It's a rare occasion indeed – I can name Michael Owen in an England squad for the first time in what feels like forever. It's Romania in the playoffs, and the games are just two weeks away, with the first leg and second leg just four days apart. He replaces Sheringham but otherwise there are minimal changes.

October is coming to a close so let's take a look at some of the transfer news. Liverpool are having a bit of a clear out, firstly Jerzy Dudek departs for Blackburn at the cost of £3m. Dudek of course would go on to famously save penalties on "that night in Istanbul" as it is almost exclusively referred to. Another stalwart of that team, Dieter Hamann, is sold to Bayer Leverkusen for £2.9m. Neither were getting regular game time at Anfield so perhaps not a big shock. This game also seems to enjoy players going back to former clubs, as Rangers shell out £4.7m to bring Charlie Miller back to Ibrox. Miller was voted SPFA Young Player of the Year in 1995 but didn't really kick on, though clearly the game is backing him for a return to the good times here.

Halloween falls on League Cup third round day and it's Arsenal who have the biggest nightmare, exiting 3-2 at the hands of Watford. Arsenal lead 2-1 with 7 minutes to go before former player Stephen Hughes scores twice to send Wenger's men packing. They aren't the only ones though, as a solitary Mark Pembridge goal sees Everton defeat Man Utd at Old Trafford, whilst John Terry is sent off as Charlton defeat Chelsea 3-1 at The Valley. There are two other Premier League sides who suffer the same fate as Arsenal and lose to lower league sides; Aston Villa are defeated 2-0 at First Division Grimsby, whilst second division

Tranmere beat Sunderland by the same scoreline. Three sides, including Leeds, will have to wait a week to play their match because of bizarre scheduling that sees the UEFA Cup fixtures played the following day.

November

Before we get to those UEFA Cup ties, my sub goalie has been appointed as manager at Hull City. David Seaman played for England during the 2002 World Cup as he and his stupid ponytail was lobbed by Ronaldinho in England's quarter final exit. Now he's a Third Division player, I can't really justify picking him in the squad, which is great news for David James, Nigel Martyn and Chris Kirkland. Be that as it may, I can't change him now, so I wonder how he'll handle playing Bristol Rovers away on the same day we host Romania.

Anyway, the UEFA Cup is over for Rangers, beaten by AC Milan over two legs. A tough draw for any team really. It's a famous night for Ipswich, who defeat Celta Vigo on penalties, Titus Bramble scoring the vital spot-kick which is incomprehensible. They are the last British side standing, as Leeds suffer a disappointing exit to SC Freiburg of Germany. A 0-0 draw at Elland Road followed by a 2-1 defeat is the end of the line. Joining Milan as obvious favourites are Barcelona and Inter Milan, who both advance with ease.

The weekend brings double injury news. David Beckham has strained a wrist. Make your own jokes, but he's now considered doubtful for next Saturday. He'll play regardless, he doesn't need wrists. Less shocking news sees Darren Anderton strain ankle ligaments and withdraw from the squad, with Ray Parlour called in. Beckham scored in Man Utd's 3-0 win over Ipswich, whilst Parlour was on target during Arsenal's 2-0 victory at Sunderland as the gap at the top remains 3 points, though Arsenal have a game in hand. Four points further back are in form Leeds, who are 1-0 winners at Goodison Park. Good news for me is Kieron Dyer is injury free and scoring goals, he actually has 5 goals in 4 games since his return from injury and will be in contention to play against Romania. His double against Tottenham is enough to snatch a point. Bolton are smashed 4-0 by fellow strugglers Derby, Ravanelli nabbing two to pile the misery on Big Sam. It is a rare occasion in Spain as both Barcelona and Real Madrid win, but so do Villarreal to maintain their top spot. Barely an eyebrow is raised in Scotland as, wait for it, both Celtic and Rangers win.

It looks like another famous European night at Anfield, England duo Fowler and Barmby opening up a 2-0 lead only for Amoruso and Tacchinardi to net 2nd half goals to earn Juve a draw. It means Liverpool drop into the UEFA Cup, that particularly stupid rule is still in place even now. Man Utd have a lot less pressure on them having already qualified, and a 0-0 draw with Lazio probably sums that up. Beckham played the whole game, to the relief of a nation. Celtic also advance, a 0-0 draw against Bayern is enough after PSV beat Copenhagen. Arsenal secure top spot with a 1-0 win over Parma, but it comes at a cost as Sol Campbell breaks a toe. Sol, man. Come on. Real Madrid survive a scare as their home defeat to Borussia Dortmund leaves them vulnerable, but Nantes' failure to beat Tirol Innsbruck sees the Spanish giants through in second. The next round group stages are drawn immediately, with Man Utd being paired with PSV, Juventus and Schalke, whilst Celtic and Arsenal are grouped together alongside Real Madrid and Roma. No thanks. Roma are unbelievable on this game, I should point out.

Campbell's injury sees him withdraw which means Jonny Woodgate is back in. Romania, of course, knocked England out of Euro 2000 when Phil Neville conceded a last minute penalty. In the real qualifying campaign, Romania were surprisingly beaten by Slovenia over two legs. Hopefully that's an omen. They are a useful side, with the likes of Dan Petrescu, Christian Chivu and a young, pre-Chelsea Adrian Mutu. It's going to be a tough match and I'd rather we were at home for the 2nd leg, but hopefully that isn't an issue.

England vs Romania 1st Leg – As it happened

It's probably a bit childish to call this revenge, but as a huge fan of Kevin Keegan I have a bit of a grudge against Romania for knocking England out of Euro 2000. Sure, it's easy to blame Phil Neville, but where will that get us? Hopefully I'll do Kevin proud here with a comfortable win before we head for Bucharest in midweek.

England have suffered a bit of a blow already, Steven Gerrard has been struggling with a strained neck all week and I was so optimistic he would recover, I haven't mentioned it until now. However here we are on game day and he's 72% fit, so he's only on the bench. Kieron Dyer is his replacement. Michael Owen is back and paired with Andy Cole, but I remain unconvinced that they are the partnership for the longer term. Romania opt for a 4-4-2, and they've left Petrescu and Mutu on the bench.

England: Wright, P Neville, As. Cole, Woodgate, Ferdinand, Dyer, J Cole, Beckham, Scholes, Owen, An. Cole. **Subs:** Martyn, Barry, Southgate, Gerrard, Heskey, Fowler, Lampard.

Romania: Stelea, Contra, Nanu, Chivu, Filipescu, D Munteanu, Cernat, C Munteanu, Ganea, Craioveanu, Ilie. **Subs:** Mutu, Lobont, Orlando, Niculae, Moldovan, Petrescu, Stoica.

With the anthems observed, it's time for kick off. Old Trafford is ready!

KICK OFF – England's Michael Owen and Andy Cole get the game started.

3 mins – A fairly tentative start, perhaps not surprising consider we are in minute 3 of at least 180. Joe Cole shoots well wide from distance.

6 mins – WOODWORK! Andy Cole gives the ball away just outside the Romania area, which shouldn't be a problem. However Cernat plays a 40 yard pass that leaves England ridiculously exposed, and Gheorghe Craioveanu running at Phil Neville. A shimmy inside and his curling effort beats Richard Wright but cannons back off the post. Blimey.

10 mins – Romania seem keen to get an away goal, understandably. They've made the better start of the two teams.

15 mins – Nothing is happening. Cat and mouse, a game of chess, cancelling each other out. Insert

other clichés here.

19 mins – This is actually so dull I'm considering how remarkable it is that Ghoerge Craioveanu has all 5 vowels in his surname.

24 mins – Here's a chance, and again it's for Romania. England are passing the ball about, some would say aimlessly, when Paul Scholes is caught on the ball by Cosmin Contra. Again the counter attack seems to catch England out, as Contra finds Ganea who cross to that man Craioveanu again, but his left footed shot goes right across the face of goal and goes out nearer the corner flag.

28 mins – England are finally in forward motion, Phil Neville's pull back picks out Michael Owen and the striker's shot is low to Stelea's right but it's pushed behind for a corner.

29 mins – Beckham's corner is well taken by Stelea, a good claim under pressure.

33 mins – **YELLOW CARD**

Stefan Nanu is an angry man. A throw-in goes the way of England and Nanu loses it with the officials, adamant it should be a Romanian ball. He's booked for his troubles.

37 mins – Dorinel Munteanu has had a great half breaking up England's play. Here he times a tackle perfectly to dispossess Kieron Dyer but his pass forward is over hit.

41 mins – Andy Cole has his first sight of goal, drilling in a low shot that looks set to nestle in the bottom corner until Contra makes a great sliding block. England could do with a goal to calm the nerves of an increasingly frustrated home crowd.

44 mins – **GOAL FOR ROMANIA! England 0 – 1 Romania (Gheorghe Craioveanu)**

We can't even blame Phil Neville for this one. Rio Ferdinand tries an ambitious pass and that man Dorinel Munteanu intercepts. He gives it to Craioveanu who leaves Woodgate on his backside and slips it beyond Richard Wright. England are in trouble now.

45 mins – **GOAL FOR ENGLAND! England 1 – 1 Romania (Michael Owen)**

A massive sigh of relief around Old Trafford as Michael Owen equalises with England's attack from the kick off. David Beckham is the architect, crossing from the right to Michael Owen who controls the ball on his chest before shooting hard and low through a defender's legs and into the corner. Phew!

HALF TIME: England 1 – 1 Romania

The only thing better than scoring before half time is letting the other team score before half time and then equalising. Probably. Be that as it may, Romania have an away goal and would certainly have taken this before the game.

KICK OFF – Romania get us back underway

46 mins – **GOAL FOR ENGLAND! England 2 – 1 Romania (Andy Cole)**

He gets the ball he scores a goal, ANDY ANDY COLE! The perfect start to the second half as a goal made in Manchester is scored at the Stretford End. Paul Scholes is the provider, skinning Dorinel Munteanu and then lifting a ball into the area where the movement of Andy Cole sees him get half a yard on FIlipescu and it is enough to give him the space to head the ball beyond Stelea. Andy or Andrew? Who cares!

50 mins – The man with all the vowels is at it again, this time Nanu strides forward down the left and his pass to Craioveanu sees the Villarreal man in a bit of space on the edge of the box. He shoots, perhaps instinctively, but Wright is ready for it and

saves easily.

52 mins – **GOAL FOR ENGLAND! England 3 – 1 Romania (Michael Owen)**

Another headed goal! Scholes again the provider, receiving the ball from Phil Neville on the corner of the area before teasing a cross in that Owen is alive to, getting in front of his man to head in England's third. Daylight.

54 mins – Old Trafford is a cacophony of noise. The half time team talk has obviously worked wonders.

59 mins – Off the bar! Phil Neville has played really well today, his right wing cross is on the head of Andy Cole but this time his header hits the woodwork and Cernat can hack it clear.

62 mins – Here's Kieron Dyer showing some of his club form. He runs with the ball and doesn't get a serious injury, before driving a shot inches wide. England's confidence is sky high right now.

64 mins – **Substitution for Romania**. Ioan Ganea, to be of Wolves in the future, is hooked and replaced by Viorel Moldovan, previously of Coventry. The midlands love a Romanian.

68 mins – Big penalty shout, Andy Cole goes down under the challenge of Filipescu but the referee makes an emphatic "no" gesture and the game goes on.

70 mins – **Substitution for Romania.** Time for another change, as Nanu is replaced by Dan Petrescu. Petrescu Is at Southampton having featured for Sheffield Wednesday, Chelsea and Bradford in previous Premier League seasons.

72 mins – The Munteanu's combine, but Catalin's shot is a lot worse than Dorinel's pass. As far as Wikipedia knows, those two aren't related.

75 mins – Beckham is the latest to try his luck, from about 25 yards he shoots with that trusty right foot but Stelea saves. The corner is flicked on by Woodgate but cleared by Chivu.

79 mins – **GOAL FOR ENGLAND! England 4 – 1 Romania (Andy Cole)**

What a wonderful finish this is. Andy Cole and Michael Owen, who some idiot wrote off as a pair pre-game, try to exchange passes but Owen's return pass looks overhit. Never to be deterred, Cole smashes a volley from a tight angle that flies into the far corner. That's a nice looking score line now for England.

82 mins – **Substitution for England**. Andy Cole may have a knock, so he is replaced by Robbie Fowler for the closing minutes.

86 mins – Beckham at it again, receiving a pass from the industrious Joe Cole before shooting a yard over the bar.

89 mins – Woodwork! England nearly get a fifth, but Owen's low shot clips the post and goes behind. 2 minutes will be added.

90+1 mins – England just keeping the ball now, the job is just about done.

FULL TIME: England 4 – 1 Romania

It is essentially half time in this World Cup playoff but England hold a heavy advantage. Romania will have to win 3-0 in Bucharest to go through, or if England score, Romania will need five. Surely England won't let that happen? Michael Owen gets man of the match and a perfect 10 rating, but let's be fair, everyone was excellent.

It's not exactly a goalfest in the other matches, Austria winning 1-0 in Belarus and Yugoslavia beating Croatia 2-0. Denmark and Sweden draw 0-0 in an all Scandinavian battle. All in all, I am happier with my result than any other.

There's not much time for anything to major to happen before the second leg, but one of our cover stars is on the move. Stefan Selakovic joins Blackburn for £1.4m from Halmstad. Selakovic wasn't a bad player by any means, he got 12 real-life caps for Sweden, but in CM01/02 he is one of the finest attacking midfielders you could pick up for under £2m. If Blackburn utilise him, they will quickly improve on their 15th place, but then again they are managed by Graeme Souness so don't bank on it.

Romania vs England – As it happened

Surely not even England can blow a 4-1 advantage? I'm not going to over complicate anything by trying to play for 0-0 or something daft like that. My theory is, if we score, they need 5. I am confident we can get away without conceding 5. One change for England, Gerrard is back to replace Dyer. It's perhaps a bit harsh on Dyer but he's not Steven Gerrard. Romania bring Dan Petrescu into the starting lineup for Ganea, which although is only one change it results in a mass shuffling of players with Contra going to the right wing and Ilie up front.

Romania: Stelea, Petrescu, , Nanu, Chivu, Filipescu, D Munteanu, Cernat, C Munteanu, Contra, Craioveanu, Ilie. **Subs:** Naghi, Tudor, Ganea,

Ciobotariu, Mutu, Dumitru, Niculae

England: Wright, P Neville, As. Cole, Woodgate, Ferdinand, Gerrard, J Cole, Beckham, Scholes, Owen, An. Cole. **Subs:** Martyn, Barry, Southgate, Dyer, Heskey, Fowler, Lampard.

The anthems are beautifully observed, and it's time to kick off. England are 90 minutes away from the World Cup or the latest chapter in qualification failure.

KICK OFF – Romania get us underway in front of nearly 65,000 people, most of which are baying for the comeback of a lifetime.

2 mins – Great start from England, popping the ball around nicely and a half chance falls to Michael Owen, but his fierce shot is parried away by Stelea. You do feel if England score that would settle it.

6 mins – Neither side have managed to grab hold of the game yet, it's a bit scrappy early on.

10 mins – Ghoerghe Craioveanu caused England problems at Old Trafford and here he is again, trying to get the better of Rio Ferdinand but his weak shot is straight at Wright. Rio did just enough there.

14 mins – The Romanians are turning the screw here. Cosmin Contra goes past Ashley Cole with remarkable ease and crosses for Adrian Ilie to loop a header over Richard Wright. It should really be a goal but Jonathan Woodgate shows wonderful positional sense to get back and hack it off the line. It's brilliant defending from the young Leeds man.

17 mins – England threaten that vital away goal again, this time it's Phil Neville with the cross and Andy Cole's glancing header has Stelea scrambling, but it is just wide.

21 mins – Joe Cole gets this all wrong. Scholes chips a ball in looking for Owen's run, but Contra heads it clear. Joe Cole's eyes light up at the prospect of lashing one on the volley but it goes many miles over the bar. Well, about 10 yards over. You get the idea.

24 mins – Scholes himself tries a curling effort this time but it is also a mile away. Lots of shots from England as they go in search of the killer goal.

29 mins – Romania are asleep as Phil Neville throws the ball 20 yards infield. That man Scholes again controls it on his thigh before hitting a volley that dips and Stelea does well to watch it and hold on. An inventive effort.

32 mins – Romania's turn to threaten now, as Contra again gets free down the right and his cross picks out our friend with all the vowels, but he's denied by a brilliant Richard Wright save. The corner is cleared with ease.

33 mins – Another Romania chance, this time Adrian Ilie's header is tipped wide by the increasingly busy Richard Wright.

34 mins – The corner is cleared but only to Contra, who whips another ball back in and Ilie again is first to it but his header flashes a couple of yards wide.

38 mins – **GOAL FOR ROMANIA! Romania 1 – 0 England (Adrian Ilie)**

The lead is reduced is two, and you can't say England weren't warned. Adrian Ilie makes a fool out of Phil Neville and earns himself space to shoot in the box on his left foot. It's a brilliant finish but hopefully not the start of something big. Having seen Ilie's threat in the air it's maybe a surprise to see him score with his feet.

42 mins – England have a corner in response, and another pinpoint Beckham delivery finds Owen loitering in the 6 yard box. His header is firm but

Stelea again makes the save. Rio Ferdinand then heads the resultant corner over the bar.

44 mins – Andy Cole! What a save though, Beckham's ball in finds Cole and his header is low and well directed but Stelea again gets fingertips on the ball. He's made some excellent saves. One added minute.

HALF TIME: Romania 1 – 0 England (England lead 4-2 on aggregate)

England have been quite good in response to going behind but Stelea is having a good game. Having said that, Richard Wright has made some top saves himself, but couldn't deny Adrian Ilie shortly before half time. It's not a worry yet but if Romania score the next goal, it's going to be tense.

KICK OFF – England kick off the second half

50 mins – Manchester United trio Neville, Scholes and Cole combine again, this time Scholes' pass finds Cole's feet and after shimmying to get himself half a yard to shoot, Dan Petrescu blocks his shot.

51 mins – Has anybody noticed David Beckham's corners are brilliant? Just everyone, right then. Beckham's corner this time finds Jonathan Woodgate, who powers a header at goal just like

he did in Berlin but this time Bogdan Stelea saves it and Romania hack it clear.

52 mins – **Substitution for Romania**. An attacking switch as Cernat is replaced by Adrian Mutu.

53 mins – At the other end, Romania have a bit of a break on but Dorinel Munteanu wastes it by curling an effort well over from long range.

55 mins – Craioveanu tries something similar to Munteanu but it is well over the bar. Romania need something more accurate.

57 mins – GOAL! No! Disallowed. Steven Gerrard, who has been very quiet, crosses for Michael Owen who is free in the area and directs his header beyond Stelea. But he's free because he's offside by a yard. Shame.

61 mins – Andy Cole tries his luck but it's just over the bar. The game is stretched which is making for a lot of chances.

64 mins – Great save from Richard Wright! Munteanu this time thinks better of shooting and he finds Craioveanu who shoots, yet again, but this time Wright shuffles over and tips it away.

65 mins – **Substitution for England.** A double change, in fact. Emile Heskey is on for Andy Cole, presumably to try and hold the ball up front for a bit, and Kieron Dyer is on for Paul Scholes. Scholes hasn't featured too much in the second half.

67 mins – Munteanu swings over a corner and Contra gets above Gerrard and powers a header towards goal, but Wright turns it away.

69 mins – **GOAL FOR ENGLAND! Romania 1 – 1 England (Emile Heskey)**

There is not a finer thing for a football manager than two substitutes combining to score a vital goal. Kieron Dyer does brilliantly, bursting past a couple of tired looking Romanian challenges before finding Michael Owen on the edge of the box. Owen crosses and Emily Heskey outmuscles his marker to direct the ball into the corner on the half volley. The team celebrate with Richard Wright, which is telling.

73 mins – Romania look defeated. They need three in 20 minutes just to force extra time. I can't see it.

77 mins – The England fans here in Bucharest are enjoying themselves now. That Heskey goal has released the pressure valve.

81 mins – A headed chance for Heskey but he puts it well wide after good work from Owen.

84 mins – It's Michael Owen's turn to miss a headed chance, he also heads wide under pressure from Contra.

87 mins – Woodwork! Craioveanu, a name I hope to never have to type again, goes on a run and after beating Kieron Dyer, he gives the ball to Contra who smashes a shot that hits the crossbar. Not your day, Romania.

90 mins – There's only stoppage time to negotiate now. Romania need 3 to force extra time, even the most negative England fan wouldn't bet on that happening now. Four added minutes.

90+2 mins – Romania still going, to their credit. Ilie shoots on the half volley but Wright saves it and more importantly holds on with plenty sniffing for a tap in.

90+3 mins – Adrian Mutu tries a bicycle kick but it goes well wide. That's got to be it now.

FULL TIME: Romania 1 – 1 England (England win 5-2 on aggregate)

ENGLAND QUALIFY FOR WORLD CUP 2002

A month later than planned, England are on the plane. It wasn't without difficulty but the end result was emphatic. Somebody get on the phone to Ant & Dec, we need a World Cup song after all.

Denmark crush Sweden 4-1 in Stockholm to secure their place in the finals, whilst Austria get a late equaliser to defeat Belarus on aggregate. Croatia can't find a way past Yugoslavia and it finishes 0-0 on the night, meaning Yugoslavia advance. The draw is on December 27th, which seems like an awful inconvenience during the Christmas period.

With that, there'll be no more International football for several months meaning we can focus just on the domestic action. The 17th November turns out to be quite the day, as Bolton record their first win of the season. They come from behind to win 3-2 at White Hart Lane with Paul Warhurst at the double. With Man Utd & Arsenal inexplicably not in action, 3rd placed Leeds have a chance to close the gap but they lose 4-1 at Leicester after having Nigel Martyn sent off. 4th placed Newcastle have no such trouble, winning the Tyne-Wear derby at the Stadium of Light 2-0, where Kevin Phillips is sent off early on for headbutting Carl Cort. A glorious day. Fulham's Jean TIgana gets the dreaded vote of confidence after his side drop to 19th following a 3-1 defeat at home to Liverpool, Heskey scoring and getting man of the match. He's cheerful. There's a shock in Scotland as Celtic surrender a 2-0 lead to only draw at Livingston, whilst Rangers stuff Dunfermline 4-0 to return to the summit. They are a point ahead but Celtic have a game in hand. Spain continues to confuse everyone, as Real Madrid draw 2-2 at Rayo Vallecano. Barcelona do at least win 1-0 at Real Zaragoza. Villarreal stay top after a 1-0 win against a much fancied Deportivo side.

The real headline from Saturday is that Aston Villa sack John Gregory. Deadly Doug strikes again and after Villa go from 2-0 up to 3-2 down at Charlton, even Paul Merson's late equaliser can't save John Gregory the sack. They sit 17th with 2 wins in 12 games, with David Ginola classed as a star player but rather oddly loaned out to Sheff Utd. Gregory actually lasted until January 2002 in real life before quitting, later taking over at Derby...who were relegated. As of this writing he's a coach in the Indian Super League. How cultured.

Back on the pitch, the Champions League second group stage is underway but Man Utd suffer a 2-1 loss in Turin. Better news elsewhere though, as it turns out I gave Roma the kiss of death but bigging them up a few pages ago. Tony Adams scores a 90th minute winner in the Stadio Olimpico to give Arsenal a crucial 1-0 win. Would you believe it? If you think that's unlikely, Celtic beating Real Madrid 2-0 with Bobo Balde winning man of the match must be right up there. But that's what happened, and a man called Leslie Middlemas was the referee. Yep.

The game of the weekend is undoubtedly Leeds vs Man Utd. Juan Veron scores an 88th minute winner which keeps Fergie's men top of the table, even though Arsenal thrash Everton 4-1. Liverpool are into the top 6 after a 2-1 win over Tottenham. It comes at a price though as Michael Owen tears a groin muscle and is out for 3 months. As England don't play again until March, I couldn't care less. Leicester are a big of a surprise package, they're 5th after winning at Ipswich, whilst Newcastle climb to third after a 3-1 win over Fulham. Bobby Robson has, somewhat surprisingly, opted to purchase Billy Dodds from Rangers. He'll be 33 in a couple of months and perhaps his goal here is the reason Jean Tigana is sacked. Celtic and Rangers both win, scoring 5 and 4 respectively, but we have new leaders in Spain. Athletic Bilbao takes advantage of Villarreal's surprise defeat at Valladolid by beating Valencia to go top. Benitez's Valencia are 15th, which must be a concern.

There are ridiculous scenes in the League Cup, as Newcastle contrive to draw 3-3 at home to Third Division Luton Town and then go out on penalties.

Bolton's brilliant season continues with a 4-0 home defeat to First Division Wolves, but Leicester win at real life winners Blackburn to mean they are the highest ranked team left in the competition at the Quarter Final stage. Their reward is a trip to Liverpool, one place below them in the league ladder. Giant killers Luton host Tottenham, with the other two ties being Tranmere vs Millwall and Wolves vs Charlton. The Scottish League cup quarter finals are on the same night, and whilst there is no shock at Celtic defeating St Mirren, Motherwell claim a penalty shootout victory over Rangers at Fir Park.

I was right, Valencia are concerned. They've sacked Rafa Benitez, meaning he probably won't forge a reputation to go to Anfield in a few years' time and win the Champions League. That's a pity, as I've had the pleasure of having Rafa manage Newcastle for over 18 months (as of this writing) and he's revitalised the entire club. I hope his digital counterpart finds success. Aston Villa however have opted for George Graham to lead them back to the glory days, or at the very least away from the bottom three. Assistant manager John Deehan took charge for one game, and he defeated Middlesbrough 3-0. John Gregory must love him.

Some transfer news to finish November, and Leeds have decided they need creativity. They spend a combined £18m on Eyal Berkovic from Man City and Nobby Solano from Newcastle. It's this kind of reckless spending that results in financial meltdown, Peter. Berkovic played for a handful of clubs in England, but never really settled anywhere. He was involved in an infamous training ground bust up with John Hartson whilst at West Ham but was a very talented playmaker on his day. Solano, by contrast, was a hugely popular figure on Tyneside and used to play his trumpet (not a euphemism) for his teammates and manager. He can play down either wing on this game but moved to full back much later in his career. Abel Xavier has moved from Everton to Villa, presumably something John Gregory started, but I'm sure it still makes Paul Gascoigne sad. Please don't go, Abel. Mark Bosnich has turned up at Derby, incredibly Jim Smith has paid £1m for him. Bosnich was a regular for Aston Villa in the 90s before being one of the many Alex Ferguson tried to replace Peter Schmeichel. He had since moved on to Chelsea where he wasn't getting a game, and at 29 could still have some good years ahead of him. Pointless memory of Mark Bosnich is that he was the goalkeeper for the Celebrity team on *The Match* on Sky One, where a team of celebrities took on a team of legends. Unfortunately, Mark got injured early on and comedian Terry Alderton ended up in goal and pulled off some unbelievable saves. That was a good show, somebody bring it back please.

December

The Premier League advent calendar has a Merseyside Derby behind door number one, and in fact it only takes a single minute for Steven Gerrard to open the scoring. Seventy odd minutes later Jamie Redknapp adds a second to make it a happy day for Houllier's men at Goodison Park. Manchester United win, for a change, beating Newcastle 1-0. Arsenal are briefly pegged back from 2-0 to 2-2 at The Riverside, but Patrick Vieira soon nips that in the bud to secure all three points. The George Graham Effect, if that is a thing, is in full flow at Villa Park as his resurgent Aston Villa beat Leeds 3-1. Ridiculous game of the day comes at White Hart Lane, where Tottenham find themselves 2-0 down to Southampton inside 20 minutes. Glenn Hoddle, determined not be undone by his former club, subs off Neil Sullivan for Kasey Keller and his side go on to win 6-3. Managerless Fulham defeat West Ham 2-1 to move 6 points ahead of bottom side Bolton, who lose 3-1 at Sunderland. In Scotland, Rangers nick a 1-0 win at Livingston thanks to Tore Andre Flo whilst Celtic beat Motherwell 3-0. It's Villarreal who lead in Spain, another nervy 1-0 win puts them one point ahead of Atheltic Bilbao, who are 3-0 losers at

Espanyol. Barcelona and Real Madrid record away wins to move to 3rd and 5th respectively. They're coming.

Fulham have poached Mark McGhee from Millwall to be their new manager. Millwall are 14th in Division 1 so it's not the most progressive of move for the Cottagers. To be fair to Mark McGhee, he won the second division last season and in real life would go on to reach the play offs in Division 1, so maybe Fulham have the inside line on this one.

Bayern Munich win the Intercontinental Cup, defeating Boca Juniors 2-1. Great. Meanwhile, in the Champions League, Arsenal win the latest battle of Britain by defeating Celtic 3-1. Manchester United are also victorious, grinding out a 2-1 win over Schalke. That's it though until February, the ridiculous scheduling of the Champions League means there are two games in this second group stage before Christmas with the next four following in February and beyond. The UEFA Cup is also on hiatus until February, however we are down to 16 after Thursday's results. Liverpool will face the Intercontinental champs in the next round after 6-0 win on aggregate against Viking of Norway, but Ipswich need a late Gary Croft goal to advance on the away goals rule against Sigma Olomouc. Inter Milan also sneak through on away goals after a 2-2 draw in

Kiev. Can you remember when commentators used to say "away goals count double" as a way to remind you that the team who scored the most away goals would advance in the event of a draw? Actually, having typed that out, I can see why. I seem to have jinxed AC Milan, who surprisingly exit at the hands of PAOK Salonika.

There's a handful of midweek Premier League games, seemingly for no reason other than to keep me on my toes. Newcastle defeat Everton 2-1 to solidify their Champions League placing, whilst bottom club Bolton draw 2-2 with Fulham in Mark McGhee's first game. It's a similar tale in Scotland, where Rangers win but Celtic don't play.

If there is anything more satisfying than an 89th minute penalty against Alex Ferguson, I don't want to know about it. Paolo Di Canio is the man on the spot, sending Barthez the wrong way and earning West Ham a point at Upton Park. Arsenal take full advantage with a 3-0 home win against Leeds, meaning they can go top of the table if they win their midweek game in hand. Newcastle stop the George Graham effect in its tracks to remain third, whilst Liverpool have snuck up into 4th courtesy of a 1-0 win over Middlesbrough. Leicester might be going well in 5th but they suffer the indignity of being only the second team to lose to Bolton, going down 3-1 at the Reebok. The Trotters are still 6 points from safety though. Rangers can only draw at home to Aberdeen, meaning Celtic's win at Kilmarnock means the Scottish League mirrors the English league in that we can have a new leader after the midweek games. It's all happening this weekend as over in Spain the top two clash, with Atheltic Bilbao comfortable 3-0 winners over Villarreal. Barcelona & Real Madrid's wins put them within striking distance of second place with their games in hand. For those wondering, Valencia appointed Luis Fernandez of PSG as their new manager.

It's no wonder everybody is knackered at Christmas, I'm exhausted just trying to keep on top of the schedule. Midweek brings us league and cup action, starting with the English League Cup. Tottenham end Luton's wonderful run with a 2-0 win at Kenilworth Road. Wolves hammer Charlton 3-0, making light of the division gap separating the teams. Tranmere defeat Millwall 3-2 in an all football league encounter. The tie of the round, in every sense, is at Anfield, where Liverpool lead Leicester 3-0 after 28 minutes. However, that just angers Ade Akinbiyi and after he scores twice to make it 3-2, a very young Damien Delaney heads in from two corners to give Leicester the 4-3 win. Football eh? The Spanish Cup also happens, tie of the round sees Real Madrid defeat league leaders Athletic Bilbao after extra time, whilst Barcelona need penalties to see off Eibar. Villarreal advance but Valencia and Deportivo bow out. Arsenal do what Man Utd couldn't and win 2-0 at Upton Park to go top of the Premier League, whilst Celtic grab a routine 3-0 win over Dunfermline to go top of the SPL.

The weekend is here again, and with just 10 days until the man dressed in red arrives, it is perhaps fitting that Arsenal keep up their momentum with a 1-0 win at Portman Road. Man Utd beat bottom club Bolton 2-0, but the top two meet at Old Trafford on Wednesday. Liverpool take 3rd spot after a Jari Litmanen hat trick gains a measure of revenge with a victory at Filbert Street, whilst Newcastle can only draw 0-0 at Middlesbrough to slip to 4th. The Mark McGhee era is lit up by a 3-1 win over fellow strugglers Derby, but a defeat for Blackburn at Tottenham costs Graeme Souness his job. Meanwhile, Chelsea can only draw 1-1 at Villa Park, and that indignity is enough to account for Claudio Ranieri. Happy holidays indeed. Glasgow draw with Edinburgh – Celtic at home to Hearts and Rangers away to Hibs both end in stalemates, whilst Barcelona are top of La Liga. Out of nowhere, their win at Sevilla lifts them above Athletic Bilbao and Villarreal, who suffer a 4-0 home reverse to a rampant Real Madrid, inspired by a new signing which we'll get onto in a moment. There are games in hand to play for Barcelona and

Real Madrid, which will be in the midweek roundup.

December 15th is a big day, as the European transfer window opens. This is before we have the January transfer window and such, and England didn't abide by it. The biggest move sees Real Madrid sign Francesco Totti for £40.5m. It's obviously been well publicised that the recently retired Totti spent his entire career at Roma; well he won't be now. Barcelona have also paid £5.75m for Roque Junior of AC Milan. A Brazilian centre half who was considered world class, until he signed for Peter Reid's Leeds in 2003/04 and was atrocious. I'm sure Barcelona will get the best out of him. Other transfers aren't as big, such as Derek McInnes moving from WBA to Newcastle for £3.3m. A quick check on our cover stars shows me that To Madeira has signed for Portugese First Division side Lleira, whilst Cherno Samba has moved to WBA for £475k but is yet to get a game.

You can imagine the build-up Sky would give to a midweek clash between Man Utd and Arsenal, jostling for position at the top of the table just a week before Christmas. The game doesn't disappoint, Arsenal take an early lead before Man Utd storm back to lead 3-1. Patrick Vieira nets what turns out to be a late consolation and Fergie's men are back at the top, by a point. 10 points down the road are Liverpool, who beat Ipswich thanks to a solitary Emile Heskey goal. They've got a game in hand too. The Old Firm meet in freezing conditions but the unlikely figure of Joos Valgaeren warms Celtic hearts with a headed winner. Celtic are now 4 points clear with a game in hand. In boring old Spain, Barcelona and Real Madrid win 1-0. Real Madrid's goal is scored by Francesco Totti, his third goal since arriving in Madrid 5 days ago.

Blackburn appoint Kenny Dalglish. Never go back, Kenny. Dalglish of course was Blackburn manager when they won the Premier League in 1994/95 and has had an ill-fated spell in charge of Newcastle since then, but it will no doubt please the fans and he isn't Graeme Souness.

Liverpool are the form team in the Premier League, Henchoz and Heskey defeat Man Utd 2-0 which opens the door for Arsenal to be Christmas number one. Thierry Henry scores twice as they ruin George Graham's latest return to Highbury. At the bottom, Bolton record their third win to climb to 11 points, whilst Southampton's home draw with much improved Fulham leaves them second bottom on 13 points. Derby County are also on 13 points after Craig Burley's winner against Tottenham gives them a much needed lift. They are just 4 points behind Aston Villa, with Charlton and Fulham a point further up the table. It's been a miserable December for Rangers, their latest disaster is a 0-0 draw with St Johnstone. Celtic win 3-0 at Dunfermline to open up a 6 point gap with an extra game to play. It's the final games of 2001 in Spain, which Fernando Morientes celebrates with a hat-trick in Real Madrid's 3-1 win over Malaga. Barcelona hold on to top spot with a 2-1 win against Tenerife.

Boxing Day is one of the finer traditions of the football fixtures calendar, despite TV continually trying to ruin it. Arsenal beat an increasingly forlorn Charlton 3-0 at the Valley, whilst Man Utd defeat also-troubled Southampton 2-0. Emile Heskey is an unstoppable freight train from hell, helping himself to two more in Liverpool's 3-1 win over Villa. Newcastle lose 2-1 at home to Ipswich, despite leading after just two minutes. Derek McInnes was sent off after 10 minutes and it was downhill from there. Chelsea are certainly taking their time appointing a replacement for Claudio Ranieri, but a 3-0 win over Leeds probably means there's no rush. It's a very good day for Derby, beating Everton thanks to Kinkladze and Ravanelli. Rangers look set to drop more points until Barry Ferguson pops up with an 88th minute winner at Tannadice, but Celtic win 4-0 to crush that joy.

It's December 27th so that can only mean one thing: The World Cup draw. A nation crosses it's fingers and for once, superstition seems to work. We're grouped with Portugal, Ecuador and Tunisia. Portugal have Figo, Nuno Gomes and various others but we have Emile Heskey so we'll let them do the worrying. Tunisia were in England's group in 1998 and were brushed aside, whilst Ecuador are a bit of an unknown quantity at this time. We'll do our homework on them. It's a decent draw. Ireland got Argentina, Poland and the USA for example, and I wouldn't have fancied Germany's group of Uruguay, Yugoslavia and Senegal.

Chelsea have appointed Bo Johansson as manager. Who? Don't all answer at once. I had to research this guy using his date of birth. It turns out, he was the Denmark manager from 1996 until 2000. He hadn't had a job since but in real life went on to manage IFK Gothenburg of Sweden and Molde of Norway. At 59, it's an odd time to be introduced to the Premier League. We'll give him the benefit of the doubt but it's a frightening insight into what could happen if you leave Ken Bates with an International phone book.

His first act is to draw 0-0 with Newcastle, leaving Chelsea in 7th and Newcastle 4th. Arsenal are able to tame Liverpool 2-1, despite Heskey scoring in a man of the match performance. A Juan Veron double keeps Man Utd on their tails, whilst it's a good day at last for George Graham. The unlikely hero is fellow George, Boateng, who scores both goals in a 2-0 win over Southampton. Kenny Dalglish had won his first two games back in charge at Ewood Park but they are thrashed 4-1 at Filbert Street. There's no games elsewhere to bring you up to date on.

Seeing as we're about to reach the end of 2001, I'll bring you up to date with some important facts and figures. Thierry Henry leads the chase for the Premier League golden boot with 14 goals, Ruud Van Nistelrooy is his closest challenger with 11. Gio Van Branckhorst has an incredible 12 assists, with Darren Anderton second with 8. In Scotland, Larrson leads the scorers chart with 16 goals, whilst in Spain Fernando Morientes has managed a modest 10 but still tops the table.

So, as the calendar changes from 2001 to 2002, most Premier League sides have played 20 games and it's looking like a two horse race between Arsenal and Manchester United with just under half a season still to play. That is ultimately how it played out in the real world, though Liverpool, Newcastle and even Leeds should be a bit closer to the top (in terms of points) by those standards. It looks like Celtic's title to lose, as they sit 6 points clear with a game in hand – and they are a couple of games ahead of the English league due to the early start. Spain have managed 17 games, so are still under half way through their season, and after a surprising first few months there is now the familiar sight of Barcelona leading from Real Madrid – though Del Bosque's side have a game in hand. Real life champions Valencia are 11th and have already dispensed with Rafa Benitez's services, so they aren't going to match their real achievements. England next play in March – a friendly with Holland – though I probably won't make the sweeping changes Sven made for a similar fixture during his tenure.

January

Happy New Year! The Premier League pendulum swings again as Arsenal can only draw at Newcastle. Whilst that isn't a bad result, Man Utd's 2-1 win at Blackburn puts them top on goal difference. Emile Heskey takes his tally for the season to 17 with two more goals, this time against Leeds, whilst there is delight for Derby as a 1-0 victory over Leicester moves them out of the relegation zone. Charlton drop in to the bottom three, losing 3-0 at home Chelsea – their 6th league defeat in a row. Alan Curbishley doesn't appear to be under any pressure though. It's as you were in Scotland, with Celtic and Rangers both winning, whilst the only game in Spain is a significant one. Athletic Bilbao come from behind to win 2-1 at Valladolid to regain top spot, though Barcelona and Real Madrid have games in hand.

It is a bit of a cliché but FA Cup 3rd round day is still one of my favourite events on the football calendar. Back in 2002, teams still took the competition extremely seriously with minimal rotation. Sadly I doubt those days will ever return in the modern game unless the winners are rewarded with Champions League football. The "David vs Goliath" tie comes at Belle Vue, Doncaster, where the Conference side host Liverpool. Jari Litmanen and Robbie Fowler put Liverpool 2-0 ahead before Doncaster pull one back to cause a frantic finale, but they can't find an equaliser that would have taken them back to Anfield. The day is not without shocks though; Curbishley's nightmare continues with a 4-0 defeat at First Division Sheffield Wednesday. Efan Ekoku netted a hat trick to the delight of 90s fans everywhere. Second Division Stoke beat Spurs 3-1, and it's even worse for West Ham as they are stuffed 4-1 at third tier Notts County. Ipswich are also beaten by a Second Division side, losing 1-0 at Bristol City. None of the Premier League high fliers are beaten though. Scotland have the weekend off but it's a chaotic day in Spain. Barcelona and Real Madrid suffer home losses allowing Athletic Bilbao to stretch their lead, which they do with a 4-0 win.

Southampton snatching a 3-3 draw against Huddersfield is not enough to save Stuart Gray his job. He is sacked shortly after the game and really, he can have no complaints. They sit 19th with 3 wins from 22 games, and even Matt Le Tissier is unhappy. They should just give him the job, really. Oh and John Gregory is back in football, appointed at Nottingham Forest. They are 21st in Division 1 though so work to be done there.

There are six midweek Premier League games, a chance to get everybody on the same number of games played. Man Utd have a fairly average record at Stamford Bridge and even with Bo Johansson in charge, Chelsea storm to a 3-1 win. That should open the door for Arsenal to go back to the top but they are surprisingly beaten at Highbury by Leicester, who move into 4th with their 1-0 win. Considering Leicester finished bottom in the real world, this is quite the turnaround. Emile Heskey scores yet again as Liverpool defeat Sunderland, they're still third but the gap to Arsenal is down to 6 points with a game in hand for Liverpool. Derby, in 17th, defeat Charlton 2-0 and yet somehow, Curbs isn't even on the insecure list. In Scotland, Celtic lose their game in hand after a surprise 2-1 loss at Tannadice.

Another weekend, another Charlton defeat. A 4-1 defeat at Fulham leaves them 5 points from safety but still in 18th position. Southampton are still managerless and slip to a 1-0 defeat at Champions League chasing Leicester, the likelihood of which is increased with Newcastle's 3-1 defeat at Leeds. Bo Johansson continues to impress after guiding Chelsea to a 0-0 draw at Highbury, which means Man Utd are now 2 points clear after beating Derby 2-0 at Old Trafford. Again there are no games in Scotland, presumably an extension of the winter break, whilst in Spain the top three all win.

Liverpool are now within 3 points of Arsenal. An impressive 3-0 dismantling of Aston Villa at Villa Park puts them within striking distance of the Gunners and just 5 points behind leaders Man Utd. Heskey netted again, for those wondering. Michael who? It's also Copa del Rey 3rd round 2nd leg day, and Barcelona bow out to Sevilla. Real Madrid have no such trouble, beating non-league Cultural 7-0 on aggregate. Even Steve McManaman scored twice.

Southampton have appointed Gary Bennett as their new manager. I know what you're thinking, why have Southampton appointed a Sunderland legend recently released by Darlington as their manager? Well, the fact is, it's not that Gary Bennett. It's actually much worse than that. For you see, this Gary Bennett played for Wrexham and Chester (amongst others) and retired in 1999.

He's never been anywhere near the Premier League, or a manager position. In an attempt to find who this Gary Bennett is I took to Google, and actually found a Gary Bennett who was on Southampton's coaching staff in 2001, but it's not him as this Gary Bennett starts the game out of work. Whether it's a research error or he just gave a cracking job interview, I don't think he's going to help.

Charlton win a game! Long live Curbs. A 2-1 win against Newcastle briefly lifts the gloom descending on The Valley. Their survival hopes are boosted further by the news that 17th placed Derby have drawn 0-0 with 16th placed Aston Villa. Man Utd and Arsenal both grind out 2-1 victories, at Fulham and Bolton respectively, but Liverpool's good run is ended by that man Bo. A 2-0 defeat at Anfield relieves the pressure on the top two. Celtic return to Saturday action with a 5-0 win against bottom club Hibs, whilst Rangers defeat Kilmarnock thanks to a Shota Arveladze double. Hands up if you'd written off Villarreal? They're back up to 2nd, their thrashing of Osasuna is just the beginning of their good day, as Barcelona slip to defeat at Deportivo (who are now 5th), whilst Real Madrid lose at leaders Athletic Bilbao. It's a strange old season in La Liga.

There are yet more La Liga games in midweek, the latest round of teams trying to catch up their games played column. The derby between Espanyol and Barcelona finishes in a 1-1 draw, which leaves Barcelona 5 points away from Athletic Bilbao. Real Madrid come from behind to win 2-1 at Deportivo, cutting the gap to Barcelona to a solitary point in the process. They still have yet another game in hand to come, I do wonder if they will ever catch up.

It's cup weekend in England and Scotland, with Arsenal, Manchester United & Liverpool enjoying simple victories against lower league sides. Bolton can barely buy a win in the league but they beat 5th placed Leicester 2-1 to advance round 5, whilst North East duo Newcastle and Sunderland both lose to Premier League opposition. Leeds account for Sir Bobby's men whilst Peter Reid has a miserable trip back to Goodison Park – Paul Gascoigne amongst the scorers in a 3-0 win. I'm sure Gazza didn't make a big deal out of scoring against Sunderland. There's a shock in Scotland as Third Division Brechin City send Premier League Hearts packing in a rollercoaster 3-2 win. Hearts had a 19 year old Craig Gordon in goal. Celtic pay the price for resting Henrik Larsson as they struggle to a 1-1 draw at home to 2nd Division Greenock Morton. They'll replay in 10 days for the right to travel to St Mirren in the next round. It's a regular league weekend in La Liga, but all of the top three win but Villarreal can only draw, so they are now 8 points off top spot.

With January drawing to a close, the last thing we need is some low key League cup semi-final first legs. But that is what we do have, as Tottenham put one hand on the trophy with a 2-0 win at Filbert Street. That man Darren Anderton scoring the crucial first goal. Tranmere and Wolves draw 1-1 at Prenton Park, which is every bit as bad as it sounds. Tranmere are 19th in Division 2 yet are one game from the final, two games from Europe. That would be something.

On the transfers front, the Premier League says goodbye to a legend when Arsenal sell Dennis Bergkamp to Roma for £5.25m. Roma had a big Francesco Totti shaped hole to fill and you'd probably say Bergkamp could give that a go. The truth is he was barely getting a game for Arsenal as he was behind Henry, Kanu and…Francis Jeffers in the pecking order. Bergkamp famously used to be unavailable for some of Arsenal's away Champions League fixtures due to his fear of flying. He presumably set off Rome by boat with all of his belongings. Another Dutchman on the move is Jimmy Floyd Hasselbaink, a victim of Bo Johansson's revolution as he is sold to PSV for £5.75m. Liverpool's aversion to squad depth continues, selling Sander Westerveld to Aston Villa for £2.7m. George Graham deems Sander a safer pair of hands than Peter Schmeichel and I suppose he is 11 years younger. Having sold Dudek and now Westerveld, Houllier takes the drastic step of signing Andy Marshall from Ipswich to provide backup to Chris Kirkland – though Pegguy Arphexad remains an option. You'll always have Pegguy.

February

Everton celebrate a new month with a takeover, a man called Graham Barlow is the new chairman and they have £6.5m to spend on new players. All debts are cleared and they didn't even have to sell Gazza. In fact they only sold Abel Xavier, which means all in all this is a success. They sit a respectable 10th in the Premier League.

The Toffees carry that good mood into their home game with Manchester United, holding on for a 0-0 draw due to the brilliance of Paul Gerrard. That is not a misprint. Arsenal take the opportunity to go joint top with a 3-0 win at struggling Southampton. Beleaguered Charlton take a creditable 0-0 draw at home to Liverpool, whilst Derek McInnes finally endears himself to Newcastle fans with the winner away at bottom side Bolton. That takes Newcastle level on points with 4th placed Leicester, who lose at Sunderland to a Lillian Laslandes double. It's another good day for Celtic, John Hartson's double leads them to a 2-0 win over Livingston but Rangers can only draw at Dunfermline. Spain continues to confuse me, top club Athletic Bilbao losing 1-0 at home to bottom side Las Palmas. Barcelona can only draw 0-0 at Alaves meaning Real Madrid are the big winners, Totti on target again as they brush Real Betis aside 3-0 to move into 2nd.

A full round of Premier League fixtures, for absolutely no reason! What a glorious Wednesday. Unless you are Arsenal, in which case you probably have that familiar sinking feeling. Mark Bosnich has the game of his life and Derby leave Highbury with a 1-0 win from an injury time free kick courtesy of the cultured right foot of Craig Burley. Man Utd ram home their advantage by defeating Charlton 3-0, but Liverpool are still 5 points behind despite their 1-0 win against Bolton. Chelsea manage to beat Southampton despite a curious incident where Frank Lampard opened the scoring but Mario Melchior and Eidur Gudjohnsen collided and picked up injuries in the same minute. The Bo Train runs on though, they're up to 6th. It's Copa del Rey time in Spain, with the big story being Atletico Madrid stunning Celta Vigo 5-1. It doesn't sound like much but Atletico are down in the 2nd Division and they're only 7th, with a 17 year old Fernando Torres to call on. Real Madrid and Real Betis both advance along with Leganes of the Segunda. Celtic play their game in hand but blow a 2-0 lead at Aberdeen to come away with a point. Their lead is still a healthy 6 points though.

When Gary Neville scores a 93rd minute winner, maybe it's written that it will be your year. That is exactly what happens at Old Trafford as Manchester United sneak a win against Sunderland, with Arsenal ready to pounce having beaten West Ham 2-1. Liverpool lose at Newcastle, and with 11 games remaining you would think it is a two horse race again. Bolton, Southampton and Charlton all lose, leaving the bottom three each separated by 5 points from the team above them. For those counting, Bolton have 12 points. Celtic are having a wobble, losing 2-1 at Hearts, opening the door slightly for Rangers who dismantle Hibs 3-0. Barcelona hammer Athletic Bilbao 4-1 which should mean Real Madrid go top of the table but instead they draw 1-1 at Las Palmas and hundreds of betting slips are torn up. Probably.

It seems like only yesterday we were waving goodbye to the Champions League as it departed for a winter break but now here we are, rekindling our love for Europe's premier club competition just two days before Valentine's Day. Arsenal face Real Madrid and what should be a really special night falls flat on its face just 4 minute in. Freddie Ljungberg is dismissed for a bad challenge on Zinedine Zidane and Arsene Wenger has the brainwave to sub Thierry Henry for Jermiane Pennant and leave Francis Jeffers on. Wenger out. Zidane scored twice and Real won 3-0. It's a loss by the same scoreline for Celtic too, away to Roma, with Gabriel Batistuta amongst the scorers. Batigol has just turned 33 but he has 24 goals in 29 games for Roma. They are a strong side, I promise. A British hat-trick of despair is completed with Man Utd losing 2-0 at PSV. David Beckham gets a 4 rating for his 77 minutes. Get them out of your system now, son.

As fate would have it, Arsenal and Man Utd clash in the 5th round of the FA Cup. As recent history would have it, Man Utd win. Ruud Van Nistelrooy scores an 82nd minute to leave most of Highbury disappointed. Result of the day comes at Craven Cottage, where cup specialists Wolves win 5-0. Temuri Ketsbaia nets a couple and presumably celebrates by kicking the advertising hoardings to smithereens. Bolton have now won as many FA Cup matches as they have league games, their 2-1 win over Aston Villa comes courtesy of a late Bruno N'Gotty goal. Middlesbrough conquer Goodison Park thanks to Dean Windass climbing off the bench to score twice in the second half. Gazza has put a transfer request in, not satisfied with his 6 appearances this season. Nobody is interested in him. It's cup day in Scotland too, and Celtic are out! Despite beating Greenock Morton in the replay, they lose 3-2 at St Mirren and deservedly so looking at the stats. Rangers can only draw at home to Livingston, as several clubs sit licking their lips hoping they exit in the replay. It's El Clasico time, but a 1-1 draw is a compromise that satisfies nobody as Athletic Bilbao win to extend their lead back to 3 points from Barcelona.

Before we get into the midweek Champions League affairs, we know who'll compete in our first final of the season. Tottenham and Leicester play out an entertaining 3-3 draw, meaning Spurs advance to Cardiff where they will play Wolves, who end Tranmere's excellent run with a 4-1 win at Molineux. Cedric Roussel, who was very average for Coventry in the Premier League a few years back, nets a hat trick. Man Utd to restore some British pride by hammering PSV 3-0 at Old Trafford, but things continue to be dismal for Arsenal, beaten by a 90th minute penalty in Madrid. Celtic fare slightly better, drawing 1-1 with Roma though Roma's equaliser comes late on from the great Cafu. The UEFA Cup participants have a few more weeks to wait yet before they are back in continental action.

Arsenal's bad month continues, more dropped points for the Gunners as Blackburn hold them to a draw at Ewood Park. Man Utd defeat Leicester to go 5 points clear. That defeat for the Foxes allows Newcastle to go back into 4th win a 3-2 with at Southampton, whilst Chelsea are up to 5th after their latest win of the BoJo era. Charlton's problems are there for all to see as they lose 2-0 at home to Bolton. It'll still take something special for any of the bottom three to mount a comeback. Michael Owen is back for Liverpool; they win 4-0 at West Ham and Owen nets the 4th after everyone's favourite man-whose-middle-name-is-Ivanhoe scores twice. He's up to 23 for the season, as Jaoan & South Korea beckons. Celtic and Rangers both win but the gap is 3 points after the Bhoys' recent troubles, whilst Barcelona are the latest team in Spain to drop the baton – a 0-0 draw at home to Real Betis looks costly thanks to Real Madrid and Athletic Bilbao enjoying away wins.

Not a lot of midweek action but what does take place is quite dramatic. The Scottish League cup semi-finals firstly see Hearts beaten by First Division Ayr. Ayr lead 3-0 at half time but despite Hearts trying to come back, it wasn't enough. They will play Motherwell in the final, who model their approach on Homer Simpson's boxing technique – getting pummelled by Celtic for 90 minutes, somehow withstanding it and then pushing down their tired opponents at the end to win. Who saw that coming? Real Madrid win their game in hand 3-0 at Osasuna to move a point behind Athletic Bilbao, and a 4 point cushion over Barcelona.

That's it for February though, there isn't even any transfer gossip to bring you. We are now entering the business end of the season.

March

It's nice to start off by handing out some accolades, even if it is a competition that inconveniences most European leagues. The African Nations Cup has been running for the past month or so and we finally have our final – Morocco vs Egypt. Morocco defeated Nigeria in the semi-finals, the Super Eagles looked a good bet with Okocha, Taribo West, Finidi George and a strike partnership of Kanu and Ade Akinbiyi. Maybe that was the problem. Egypt meanwhile knocked out Sierra Leone in the semi-finals, a 19 year-old Mido doing most of the damage with two goals. The final though was dominated by Morocco, despite their lack of household names. Not even a Youssef Chippo or a Mustapha Hadji in the squad. But well done nevertheless. Our World Cup opponents Tunisia didn't make it out of their group, actually losing to both Egypt and Morocco after beating Liberia. I remain confident of getting the better of them.

What is it about Middlesbrough for Manchester United? The pupil has got one over the teacher as Stevie Mc leads his side to a 3-1 win at the Riverside, the icing on a bizarre cake being Dean Gordon's 35 yard free kick. Thierry Henry's 29th and 30th goals of the season help Arsenal to a 3-0 win over Tottenham to reignite the title race. The top two meet again at the end of March. Elsewhere, Liverpool beat Southampton to consolidate third, though Michael Owen has sprained an ankle. Newcastle throw away a 2-0 lead at home to Derby and lose 3-2 to drop to 6th – Chelsea taking 4th and Leicester 5th after both sides enjoy handsome home wins. Bolton are off the bottom! They beat West Ham 2-0 thanks to Rod Wallace and Paul Warhurst meaning Southampton now prop up the division. Rangers and Celtic play out the dullest Old Firm derby ever at Ibrox, a 0-0 draw probably pleases Celtic more than their opponents. Las Palmas are having a great time throwing spanners in the works over in Spain, this time a 4-2 win over Barcelona leaves the Catalan giants 8 points off the top. Once again their defeat is compounded by wins for Athletic Bilbao and Real Madrid.

I receive a news article that Real Madrid's fans are livid – a 1-0 home defeat to Celtic the cause but they are still top of their group with a game to go as Arsenal and Roma draw 0-0 at Highbury. With Arsenal and Celtic tied on 7 points it is excellent news that they will face each other in the final group game at Celtic Park. Man Utd draw 0-0 at home to Juventus, which leaves them third in the group and requiring a win over Schalke next time out. If Juventus beat PSV all three sides will have 10 points and some crazy head to head tiebreakers will come into play. I'm pleased I only have a watching brief. The UEFA Cup is back and the fourth round sees us wave goodbye to Ipswich, beaten by Fiorentina on away goals. Liverpool win 3-0 in Munich to send Bayern packing whilst other favourites Barcelona and Inter both advance.

The FA Cup has reached the last 8, which seems to have flown by but it is the end of the line for cup specialists Wolves, beaten 2-1 by holders Liverpool. Also through to the last 4 as league leaders Manchester United, who hammer Leeds 4-0. All the goals are scored in the opening 35 minutes after a devastating spell from the Red Devils, and it looks like they are coming into form at the right time. As usual. Chelsea's remarkable turnaround continues with a 5-1 demolition of Middlesbrough whilst Bolton's fanciful run is ended by Man City, the only remaining football league representative. Having said that, they are managed by Kevin Keegan and sit second in Division One, so you wouldn't bet against them swapping places with their opponents in the near future. It's cup day in Scotland too, with overwhelming favourites Rangers securing their spot in the last four with an easy win over 3rd Division Brechin. Aberdeen join them after an entertaining 5-3 win over Dundee Utd, whilst Falkirk beat fellow first division side Raith Rovers. Celtic's conquerors St Mirren will need a replay against Dunfermline after a 2-2 draw. Spain brings a fantastic day where the top three all manage 1-1 draws away from home against mid-table opposition. Still 10 games to go over there.

I'm invited to name my England squad for the friendly with Holland, which is in two weeks. Before that though, I'm informed of my group for Euro 2004 qualifying, which isn't something I'll have to contend with in this book but for those wondering, we face Denmark, Finland, Slovenia, Latvia and Faroe Islands. Back to the immediate issues though and Sol Campbell is recalled after getting over his toe injury, he's in at the expense of Gareth Barry. Michael Owen will be touch and go but my desire to pair him and Heskey means he's in, and we'll wait and see how his various injuries are. A nice feature of this game greets me a few days later, as the press are writing off England's chances in the World Cup. I'm invited to respond and I tell them we will be in the final reckoning and to just chill out, I can't be doing with 3 months of this.

The final group games of the Champions League can be complicated affairs but it makes it a lot easier when one of the teams who need to win suffer a 1-0 defeat to a team already eliminated. Man Utd's 1-0 loss away to Schalke looks harsh looking at the stats but regardless, they are out and Juventus advanced with PSV. Arsenal win the vital game at Celtic Park, Henry's double gets them three precious points and the Gunners top the group as a result of Roma beating Real Madrid. Real Madrid still go through in second place and will go up against Lazio in the last 8. Arsenal face Borussia Dortmund, where we find Jens Lehmann, Tomas Rosicky and big Jan Koller.

Sol Campbell twisted a knee in that win against Celtic but has decided to fight on for his country, but he's extremely doubtful for the Holland game. So you can imagine how pleased I am when Rio Ferdinand damages a foot and is ruled out for three weeks, including the upcoming game. Jamie Carragher is called up in his place, but I'm a bit worried about his lack of pace. He is versatile though, comfortable across any position in the back four, holding midfield and the Sky Sports studio.

Barry Hayles might have just ensured the Premier League title stays in Manchester. The Jamaican striker scores the winner as Fulham defeat Arsenal, which coupled with Man Utd's 2-1 win over Aston Villa gives Ferguson's men a 5 point cushion again. Liverpool lose 1-0 at Derby, who have shot up to 13th, but Houllier has nothing to worry about as they are still 8 points ahead of Chelsea, who win 4-1 at White Hart Lane. Newcastle win 3-1 at Ewood Park to keep their top 4 hopes alive, but Bolton's 3-1 defeat at Southampton leaves them 12 points from safety. 18th placed Charlton do manage a win though, leaving them 5 points from 17th placed Aston Villa. All of Rangers' recent good work is undone in a rough afternoon in Aberdeen, a 1-0 defeat leaves them 6 points behind Celtic who smash Kilmarnock 5-0. It's as you were in Spain as all the top three all record home wins.

It annoys me a little bit that the UEFA Cup does not run in sync with the Champions League, especially as the Quarter Final second legs are just two days before an International game. Liverpool hold a 2-0 advantage over inter Milan as they head to the San Siro but fall behind on the night to an early goal from Christian Vieri. Jari Litmanen scores on the stroke of half time and even though Sergio Conceicao scores in the second half, Liverpool are through comfortably in the end. They'll meet

Barcelona next, who saw off Bordeaux over two legs. The other semi-final will pit Fiorentina against Shakhtar Donetsk. The Ukranian side dismantled Olympiakos 4-1 on aggregate, whilst Fiorentina – managed by Roberto Mancini – see off Club Brugge.

With that, we're back in the International bubble. I won't bring you minute by minute of a friendly as that's too much even for me, but I ring the changes for Holland's visit. There's a debut in goal for Chris Kirkland, who has conceded just 14 goals in 26 league games for Liverpool. Gate's Wood & South are my centre halves, and we give Kieron Dyer a chance in the hole with Scholesy a sub. Heskey partners Andy Cole up front as it would be stupid to risk Michael Owen gives his propensity to pick up injuries. It's all about experimentation, and that's what I tell the lads when we are 2-0 down at half time having not managed a shot. Luckily for me, Robbie Fowler emerges from the bench for the ineffective Heskey (5 rating) to pull one back before Joe Cole equalises in the 83rd minute. We will take it. David Beckham lasted 3 minutes before suffering a "potential foot injury," which turns out to be strained ankle ligaments rather than the dreaded metatarsal that curtailed his preparation in reality. All I learned from this match is that Chris Kirkland isn't particularly good and Emile Heskey is infuriating. We play Spain in a month; I must sack whoever arranges these things.

The final weekend in March brings the match we've all been waiting for, as Man Utd visit Highbury. The unlikely figure of Kanu scores the winner to breathe new life into Arsenal's title hopes, a good time to get his 7th goal of the season. Charlton put the cat amongst the pigeons in the battle for survival, winning a proverbial six pointer 1-0 at Villa Park, an 18 year old Swedish striker called Pagguy Zunda getting the winner. They signed him for £210k, I've never heard of him but Sweden is full of unknown gems on this game. Southampton can only draw to leave themselves in deep trouble, but Bolton don't play. Why? Because their would-be opponents Tottenham Hotspur are in League Cup final action, taking on Wolves. In a ridiculous turn of events, Wolves win 2-0, meaning the side 10th in Division One will be in Europe next season. I haven't been calling them cup specialists for nothing. It's as you were in Scotland and Spain, all five teams involved in the title races notch victories.

As March draws to a close, so too does the transfer deadline in England. We're not quite in the "slamming shut" era and with the deals that take place, it's not hard to see why. Arsenal pay £3m for the services of Gerald Sibon of Sheffield Wednesday. He's scored 6 in 18 for promotion chasing Wednesday, I can't explain why Wenger has picked him but here we are. Bobby Robson continues to purchase some odd players, opting for Albert Ferrer and Quinton Fortune from Chelsea & Manchester United to try and beef up the Champions League qualification push. Chelsea, in a similar position, sign Darren Moore from WBA. It's not yet April fool's day.

There are 7 games to go in England and Spain, whilst there are 6 in Scotland with just one more before the SPL splits into two leagues of 6.

April

British Summer Time brings Champions League quarter finals, finally out of the two group stage hell we have been stuck in since last September. The first legs are all won by the home sides, some more handsomely than others. Arsenal are Britain's last hope but they have it all to do after losing 2-0 away in Dortmund. Tony Adams got sent off which didn't help. Real Madrid are humiliated 4-1 by a rampant Lazio side, a certain Diego Simeone getting a goal and the man of the match award. PSV defeat Ajax 2-0 in an all Dutch clash whilst Juventus beat Panathinaikos 3-1, renewing their rivalry from the first group stage. Thankfully, the UEFA Cup is back in sync albeit a round ahead as the semi-final first legs are played. Jamie

Redknapp scores a vital away goal in Liverpool's 2-1 loss in the Nou Camp, but it is a much quieter affair in Donetsk as Shakhtar and Fiorentina draw 0-0.

It's a punctured Premier League fixture list due to the FA Cup semi-finals involving Manchester United, Chelsea and Liverpool. Arsenal miss the chance to go top of the table even temporarily with Thomas Gravesen earning Everton a point at Goodison after Ljungberg's opener. Blackburn hammer another nail in Bolton's Premier League coffin with a 6-1 win in a Lancashire derby at Ewood Park, whilst Charlton miss the chance to escape the bottom 3 with a 2-2 home draw with fellow strugglers Southampton. Newcastle take advantage of Chelsea's Saturday off by winning 3-0 at Fulham and moving back into 4th. Obviously it was courtesy of a Billy Dodds hat trick. It's an exceptional weekend for Athletic Bilbao, winning away at Tenerife whilst Real Madrid and Barcelona can only draw. It puts the Basque side 5 points clear with 6 to play. Rangers and Celtic both win in the last fixtures before the SPL splits into two leagues of 6, with the top 6 and the bottom 6 engaging in separate round robin formats for the remainder of the season.

Two awards are handed out – one very expected and the other rather less so. Thierry Henry is the

English Players Player of the Year, having scored 32 goals in all competitions. Ruud Van Nistelrooy is second and Juan Veron is third. The English Players Young Player of the Year award goes to Damien Delaney of Leicester. Yes, the same Damien Delaney who plays centre half for Palace. As a 20 year old, he was seen as a central or left sided player comfortable in defence or midfield. I doubt you'd get him playing centre midfield now. Joe Cole is runner-up and Julio Arca third.

The FA Cup semi-finals are played at neutral club venues, which in my opinion is the way it should be. Nobody should be excited to go to Wembley for a semi-final, it's not right. Anyway, Man City vs Liverpool is played at Ewood Park and Emile Heskey has one of his good days and scores twice as Liverpool win 4-2. Jamie Carragher also scores. Chelsea vs Man Utd is a high profile clash, played at Hillsborough, and it's perhaps surprising that Chelsea are comfortable 2-0 winners after two first half Gianfranco Zola goals. Chelsea were real life runners up so they'll get a chance to put that right, albeit against different opposition. Liverpool are of course the holders at this point, so they're on the verge of defending their trophy.

Arsenal fans vigorously celebrate on Wednesday as Robbie Keane of Leeds smashes in an injury time equaliser at Old Trafford. It means their lead at the top remains just two points. Liverpool suffer a surprise 4-3 loss at Tottenham, having been 4-1 down on the hour. That means Liverpool are back to 7 points adrift of Arsenal, but 8 points ahead of Chelsea, who return to 4th after winning away to Sunderland. The Copa del Rey semi final first legs see home wins for both Atletico and Real Madrid, which would be the final of choice for the neutral I'm sure. In Scotland, St. Mirren continue their giant killing run by beating Aberdeen in the semi-finals. They'll have one final giant to slay as they face Rangers in the final next month.

Robbie Fowler has torn a groin muscle ruling him out for 2 months. It'll be touch and go to see if he makes the tournament, but I'd bet not at this stage. He's obviously out of the Spain game which I'm trying to name a squad for now. Michael Bridges is in good form for Leeds and his reward is replacing Fowler, whilst his club team mate Rio Ferdinand is back from injury. He replaces Wes Brown who can hardly get a kick for Man Utd.

Ipswich are the latest team to do Arsenal a favour as they earn a draw against Man Utd at Portman Road. Alun Armstrong had actually given his side the lead before Dwight Yorke equalised in the second half. Arsenal edge to a 1-0 win over Sunderland to leave the top two level on points and goal difference, with Man Utd sitting top thanks to a superior goals scored column. If the top of the table is building up to a dramatic conclusion, it's quite the opposite at the bottom. Bolton lose, again, to leave themselves 12 points adrift with 15 to play for. Surely there is no way back for Big Sam from here. Southampton are only two points better off and therefore in similar strife, whilst 6 points up the table are Charlton, whose heavy loss at Middlesbrough leaves them 4 points from safety. Chelsea remain two points ahead of Newcastle in the chase for 4th after both sides enjoy home wins. Rangers have cut the gap to 4 points after grinding out a 1-0 win at Livingston, whilst Celtic have a rough day, blowing a 2-0 lead at home to Aberdeen to draw 2-2 and finishing the game with 9 men. It's as you were in Spain, the top three all winning emphatically, meaning Bilbao maintain their 5 point lead.

The midweek fixtures are bad news for Arsenal. Not only are they eliminated from the Champions League despite a 2-1 win on the night against Dortmund, but Man Utd defeat Chelsea 2-0 to regain their three point lead – though Arsenal will have a game in hand in the weeks to come. It's also a bad night for Bolton and Southampton, who are both relegated by virtue of Bolton's 1-0 defeat to 17th placed Fulham. Charlton can only manage a 1-1 home draw with Derby leaving them 6 points adrift with 4 to play, teetering on the brink.

Newcastle can't take advantage of Chelsea's defeat, a 1-1 draw at Goodison Park leaving them a point adrift in the battle for 4th. Joe Cole has sprained an ankle in West Ham's 1-0 loss at Tottenham, so Owen Hargreaves in bumped up from the Under 21's. Liverpool bow out of the UEFA Cup, peppering the Barcelona goal but they can't find a way past Roberto Bonano and a 0-0 draw means Barcelona advance. They'll face Shakhtar Donetsk in the final after they win 1-0 in extra time after 180 goalless minutes against Fiorentina.

Arsenal's results give me the impression they are exhausted. Their 1-0 win over Middlesbrough is Thierry Henry's 50th appearance of the season but it is Patrick Vieira who grabs the goal. Chelsea contrive to lose 4-3 at home to Leicester – Akinbiyi at the double – but for the second weekend in a row Newcastle can't take advantage. They face Man Utd in front of the TV cameras but Derek McInnes is sent off (again) for two yellow cards after just 13 minutes and a solitary Ryan Giggs goal wins a dour game. Charlton lose at Ipswich and Fulham get a point at West Ham. The game is almost up for Curbs. Liverpool win the Merseyside derby 1-0 thanks to a very early Jari Litmanen goal, but Michael Owen limps off with strained knee ligaments. He's out for 3 weeks and the World Cup squad is about a month away, just wrap him up in cotton wool for goodness sake. The lead is down to 2 points in Spain, as Bilbao lose at 4th placed Villarreal whilst Real Madrid win at Espanyol. Barcelona can only draw at Rayo Vallecano, leaving them 7 points adrift of 2nd place. Celtic and Rangers both win, so the game remains 4 points with 3 to play.

It's time to welcome Spain to Old Trafford, and I've decided to name a more full strength line-up with this being the last friendly before we face Portugal in Yokohama on June 17th. Alan Smith was called up to replace Owen but he'll have to be content with a place on the bench, with Dyer in for Joe Cole with Scholes in the hole. Steven Gerrard isn't fully fit, so it's another chance for Frank Lampard, with Heskey and Andy Cole up front. For once, it looks like the right decisions have been made as Lampard scores twice and Kieron Dyer adds a third. And yes, Spain did get two back but I'd started making subs by then so it doesn't really count. A 3-2 win is a 3-2 win, and you know this Frank Lampard fella might be the future. The icing on the cake would have been Bridges' debut goal from the bench, but the linesman had the nerve to disallow it. See you in Japan.

The pendulum swings back in Man Utd's favour. They secure a 1-0 win over Liverpool and then watch on as Arsenal can't find a way past Sander Westerveld in the Aston Villa goal, a 0-0 draw not much use to Wenger as they fall 5 points adrift. Charlton score a late winner against Blackburn which coupled with Fulham losing 3-2 at home to already relegated Southampton gives them a slight sniff of survival. Chelsea come from behind to win late on at Middlesbrough, which takes the gloss off Newcastle's 4-1 win at Leicester in the race for the Champions League. If Celtic could choose one way to win the SPL, I think a 5-0 home victory over Rangers would feature fairly high in the list. The fifth is Celtic's 100th league goal of the season as the title is wrapped up with two games to spare. In Spain, Bilbao hold on to their 2 point cushion as both they and Real Madrid record home wins.

With just two games to go, the calendar ticks over to May...

May

Arsenal's game in hand is away to Leicester City, who sit 6th in the table but have shipped a few goals recently. Patrick Vieira gives a captain's man of the match performance and notches in the first half, with sub Gerald Sibon adding the second late on. The gap is back to two points. The Champions League has semi-final action on the same evening, Lazio putting a big marker down as potential winners with a 4-0 thrashing of Borussia Dortmund. Juventus beat PSV 1-0 to leave the second leg very much in the balance. David Trezeguet netted the goal, who scored the winner at Euro 2000. We will have the Atletico vs Real final as both come through their Copa del Rey second legs. Atletico Madrid have shot up to 2nd in the Segunda, so promotion looks almost assured anyway ahead of a mouth-watering local derby cup final.

Man Utd retain the Premier League! They thrash already relegated Bolton 5-1 at The Reebok and put the ball firmly in Arsenal's court. The Gunners lead Ipswich 2-0 at Highbury thanks to two Kanu goals, before Thierry Henry is sent off on 29 minutes for a two footed tackle on Titus Bramble. Does not compute. With Henry dismissed and tired Arsenal a man light, Ipswich go on to win 3-2 with Dutchman Martijn Reuser getting the winner. It ends a thrilling title chase at the second last hurdle, which I think is a reasonable return in terms of entertainment value. Chelsea and Newcastle both win to send the battle for the final Champions League place to the last day, but Charlton are finally relegated. Fulham's defeat at Derby had given the Addicks some hope, but a 2-1 defeat at Leeds is the end of their Premier League stay. The title race in Spain continues to thrill, with Real Madrid losing at Malaga. Athletic Bilbao have the tough trip to Deportivo and will probably take the 1-1 draw that follows, leaving them 3 points ahead with two to play. Rangers end their season with defeat at Aberdeen whilst Celtic win 3-0. That's all academic now. Hibs are relegated with 34 points, to be replaced by St Mirren, who have Christopher Wreh (formerly of Arsenal) leading the line.

Who had money on a PSV vs Lazio Champions League final? That's what we have, as Lazio unsurprisingly defend their 4-0 lead in Germany with a 0-0 draw, but very few people would predict PSV beating Juventus 4-0. Jimmy Floyd Hasselbaink and Mateja Kezman, Chelsea past and future score twice apiece to blow the Italian giants away. The final is in Glasgow in a few weeks.

This is one of those seasons where the FA Cup final isn't the final fixture of the season. I am a traditionalist but we'll let it slide. In real life, Chelsea lost 2-0 to Arsenal in the "it's only Ray Parlour" final, but here under Bo Johansson they are a different proposition, beating Liverpool 3-2 in a thoroughly entertaining game. Emmanuel Petit gets the winner, and blue is once again the colour. Elsewhere, Bilbao fluff their lines, losing 2-1 at home to Valladolid. Real Madrid edge Deportivo 1-0 to take the two sides level on points but Bilbao remain top due to their superior head to head record. Oh Spain, you and your crazy rules. Barcelona beat local rivals Espanyol 4-0, which should be the perfect warm up for the UEFA Cup final.

What do I know? Barcelona lead 1-0 early on but trail 2-1 at half time. They look set to lose until Patrick Kluivert equalises in injury time. It should spur Barcelona on to greater things but instead they concede to Andrey Vorobey and lose 3-2 after extra time. There will be no trophy in Barcelona this season. That takes us to the last day of the season in both England and Spain, where there is decidedly more to play for in Spain than in England.

Jupp Heynckes will never need to buy a drink in Bilbao again! His side have won La Liga, a late equaliser at Alaves proving to be enough as Real Madrid slip to a 2-0 defeat away at Valladolid. Heynckes, in his second spell at the club, has lifted his side from a real life 9th placed finish and performed well above expectation. Valencia recovered to finish 7th but they are nowhere near the Champions they actually were. The triumph is no doubt made sweeter by the fact Heynckes was Real Madrid manager in 97/98, winning the Champions League but being binned for his lack of domestic success.

The only thing to be decided in England was that final Champions League spot, which Chelsea comfortably seal with a 3-0 win at Ipswich. Mikael Forssell scores his 20th and 21st of the season – just one would have done against Germany back in October but it all worked out in the end, I suppose. Henry's suspension allows Ruud van Nistelrooy to net twice on the final day and pinch the golden boot, though Henry at least finishes with the highest average rating (8.20).

We're into final territory now, starting with the Champions League final. Lazio defeat PSV 1-0 thanks to Gaizka Mendieta's free kick on the hour mark. Mendieta had cost Lazio £29m in the summer and whilst he has obviously paid for himself here, in reality he ended up at Middlesbrough. Like Mendieta, Lazio had a very underwhelming Champions League campaign, finishing bottom of their group and being eliminated.

There are no further fairy tales in Spain, Real Madrid take out their anger on local rivals Atletico by thumping them 3-0 in the Nou Camp. It doesn't sound surprising and when you see the goal scorers are Zidane, Figo and Roberto Carlos, it's even less of a shock. Nothing can prepare you for St Mirren winning the Scottish Cup though. That man Christopher Wreh scores early on and Rangers batter the Buddies for 77 minutes but Flo, Mols, Arveladze and Charlie Miller can't find a way through and it's St Mirren who round off a miserable season for Rangers. Another of our cover stars has turned up at Rangers, but seeing as Kim Kallstrom is an unused sub and Mark Kerr made 11 appearances all season, it's fair to say Dick Advocaat wasn't willing to indulge us in nostalgia. Portsmouth win the playoff final, securing a debut season in the Premier League ahead of schedule and before Harry Redknapp has rocked up. West Brom are promoted as champions and Coventry join them in the automatic places. Real life champions Man City finish 5th and lose to Portsmouth in the playoff semi-finals. Kevin Keegan's position is said to be insecure. Somebody hide those big headphones.

To draw a line under the domestic season, we get the Premier League team of the season announcement. Nobody is surprised to see Henry and Van Nistelrooy up top but Damien Delaney on the left wing and Steve Elliott of Derby at centre half is a bit niche. England captain Beckham makes the bench. Spain don't seem to bother with such nonsense, possible explaining their success as a footballing nation, but Scotland name Henrik Larsson as a central midfielder alongside Charlie Miller with Sutton & Hartson up front and Steve Guppy at left back. Guppy's 33 and played 56 times, if he was ten years younger he'd be on my

England radar. But he isn't.

World Cup

June brings us into a section so important we've given the tournament the chapter heading. It's time to name a 23 man squad that will fly out to Japan & South Korea. Some rather suspect scheduling will see us start with a game in Yokohama, then fly to Seoul for our second game 6 days later and then finally to Daegu for the final game. I'm half expecting the last 16 to be played back at Old Trafford if we get that far. Anyway, enough of my grumbling, I've got people to disappoint.

Wayne Bridge is the first to receive my bad news phone call. He's been in the squad by default throughout, but I need a space to accommodate Carragher's versatility, and as both he and Phil Neville can cover Ashley Cole, Bridgey is out. I'm sure he'll fight back by marrying a pop star and winning over the public in a reality TV show, but for now, it's back to relegated Southampton for him.

Ray Parlour and Lee Bowyer have both been taking up a space for a while now, the normal squad size is 26 so with three needing to be cut from the outset, these two were in trouble. Steve

McManaman and Nick Barmby survive but we'll have to manage with Parlour and Bowyer.

The final decision comes up front, where Robbie Fowler has made a fool of my diagnosis and made a full recovery. He joins Owen, Heskey and Andy Cole as the strikers in the squad, meaning both Bridges and Smith miss out. In a huge contrast to Sven's selection dilemma, I have no injuries to my first choice players to contend with.

Let me take you back to the summer of 2002. As the World Cup approached, there was a genuine feeling that England had a chance of going deep into the tournament. Captain David Beckham was a global superstar, but a broken metatarsal badly affected his preparation and although he made the opening game against Sweden, there were question marks over his match fitness.

There was also a problem that England had been drawn in the so-called 'group of death' along with Sweden, Nigeria and old enemies Argentina. The second group game against the Argentinians was billed as Beckham's chance for revenge after his red card against them in the 1998 World Cup, however Beckham's popularity had flipped 180 degrees since then, being made the England captain and then of course *that* goal against Greece. Here though, the group is much kinder, even if we haven't had Beckham's free kick of a certain 5-1 win in Germany.

Speaking of which, England have a genuine World Class centre forward in Michael Owen. Having won the Ballon d'Or in 2001, Owen comes into the tournament as the best player in the world. It is not very often an Englishman can say that, and I feel Owen's talents have been somewhat forgotten about due to his (in my opinion) poor punditry and career choices. But after his famous solo goal in the 1998 World Cup, Owen continued to bang them in for club and country, helping Liverpool to the UEFA Cup as well as an FA Cup and League cup along the way. For reasons nobody is really sure of, Sven used to like to play Heskey as a left winger so Darius Vassell start the tournament up front with Owen. But that wasn't the only problem.

Injuries picked Sven's squad apart. Gary Neville was relegated to punditry duties in the ITV studio after breaking a foot, to be replaced by Danny Mills. Steven Gerrard was next to go, he required surgery on a groin injury that had been troubling him for the closing months of the season. Liverpool team mate Danny Murphy was expected to replace Gerrard in the line-up but he also suffered the dreaded metatarsal injury, prompting Trevor Sinclair to be promoted from standby. Tricky Trev would end up playing the majority of the tournament on the left wing, with Heskey joining Owen up front.

Sinclair was originally on standby for Kieron Dyer, who had been injured from a bad tackle on the final day of the season. Dyer did make the final squad but was only used as a substitute. Opportunity certainly knocked for West Ham's Sinclair, who ended up replacing the injured Owen Hargreaves during the game against Argentina, whilst Nicky Butt also made the most of his chance as he went on to receive recognition from Pele as one of the players of the tournament.

What I'm saying is, the Golden Generation didn't get a chance here to show us what they really could do. Is a quarter final defeat to Brazil their limit? Will Gerrard's return be the missing ingredient? Does picking a goalkeeper without a stupid ponytail inspire an entire defence? We're going to find out – and you won't have to get up at 7am to watch it.

The tournament gets underway with holders France – such was the tradition at the time – facing Russia. France avoid an embarrassing defeat this time but do only manage a 1-1 draw as the Russians do what most Premier League defences couldn't and cope with Thierry Henry. The other game in Group A sees Costa Rica defeat Paraguay

1-0, in a less than classic start to a World Cup.

In Group B we find Turkey, who would actually go on to finish 3rd and were surprise packages in the finals. They're off to a good start here with a 1-0 win over South Africa thanks to Hakan Sukur, who has since gone into Politics in his homeland. Co-hosts Japan are also in group B but they lose 2-1 to two Pavel Nedved goals for the Czech Republic.

South Korea will be disappointed to throw away a leading position twice in their 2-2 draw with Belgium. The co-hosts also have Spain to contend with, who defeat Mexico 2-1. This is a few years before Spain would become the dominant force of European football and still very much in the era where they would fail to live up to their reputation. Raul's late winner might help to change that.

Brazil get their campaign underway, they are overwhelming favourites to win Group D and a 2-1 win over Austria is a good start. Ronaldo and Elber got the goals but it is a squad of immense attacking talent including marauding full backs Cafu and Roberto Carlos. In this group we also see Nigeria defeat India 5-0. India vs Brazil has a real chance of being double figures, I'm afraid to say.

You'll never beat the Irish! Unless you're Argentina, in which case a Juan Veron double will do just that. Ireland will hope to have better luck against Poland and the USA, in what is a bit of a tough call for second place. Poland managed to defeat the USA 1-0 to put themselves in the driving seat but there are plenty of matches still to play.

We are in Group F, where Tunisia beat Ecuador 2-0 to lay down an early marker. We'll face Portugal in a couple of days, the scheduling typically has us going last for no real reason. Germany are underway in Group H though, an uninspiring 0-0 draw with Yugoslavia means they are playing catch up with Uruguay, who defeat Senegal 3-1 to top the group.

Group G is where we find Italy, who are comfortable 2-0 winners over Denmark. From my experience, whoever beats Italy will go very far in the tournament. China and Cameroon complete the group with an entertaining 2-2 draw.

Time for the main event...

Portugal vs England – World Cup Group F

After what feels like an eternity since the playoff win over Romania in November, followed by having to watch every other team in the tournament get their campaigns underway, it's finally England's turn. It's definitely the toughest clash in the group for both teams, and also a re-run of their opening group game from Euro 2000. We all know how that ended…

In the here and now at the Yokohama International stadium there isn't a Dennis Wise or Martin Keown in sight, though it has to be said most of that squad are still here. David Seaman isn't, he decided managing Hull was the way forward and Richard Wright has grabbed his opportunity with both hands (pun intended) and has in fact just been voted the third best goalkeeper in Europe. Seaman's lads lost in the Division 3 playoffs, so swings and roundabouts. The England team is almost as you'd expect, though Lampard is preferred to Gerrard in the central midfield role. The Chelsea man has 3 goals and 3 assists in that position whereas Gerrard has directly contributed nothing, so the decision is made. I've also opted for Gary over Phil at right back, and Andy Cole to partner Michael Owen.

England: Wright, G Neville, Campbell, Ferdinand, Ash. Cole, Lampard, Beckham, J. Cole, Scholes, Owen, An. Cole. **Subs:** Kirkland, Carragher, Woodgate, Gerrard, Dyer, Heskey, Fowler.

Portugal's star man is Luis Figo, who scored a splendid goal in the aforementioned Euro 2000 clash. He has since swapped Barcelona for Real Madrid and had a pigs head thrown at him, but his hair is still jet black, and isn't that the main thing? He's on the right wing here, with Paulo Sousa and Rui Costa a formidable central duo. Nuno Gomes, another Euro 2000 scorer, is up front with Luis Boa Morte of Fulham. Salon favourite Abel Xavier is at right back, which can only help us.

Portugal: Ricardo, Xavier, Litos, Fernando, Rui Jorge, Figo, Rui Costa, Paulo Sousa, Edgar, Boa Morte, Nuno Gomes. **Subs:** Helder, Nuno, Sergio Conceicao, Joao Tomas, Helder, Beto, Jorge Costa

The national anthems are impeccably observed, the waiting is finally over. It's World Cup time!

KICK OFF – Owen and Lampard get the match started, England kicking towards the Portugal fans in the first half.

4 mins – Nothing has happened so far. Both sides are sizing each other up but there are some nerves out there.

8 mins – David Beckham tries from distance but it's well over the bar. It's a shot, even if it's nowhere near.

11 mins – Still both sides cancel each other out. We need something to spark this game into life.

16 mins – **GOAL FOR PORTUGAL! Portugal 1 – 0 England (Boa Morte)**

There's that spark I was talking about. England fall behind to one of the players they should know the most about. Boa Morte skins David Beckham for pace on the half way line to have a clear run at Campbell. Sol comes charging in and the Fulham man leaves him for dead before finishing smartly into the roof of the net. Work to do for England, but a wonderful goal.

20 mins – Ashley Cole hits a shot that Abel Xavier does well to block, but Cole bursts onto his on rebound and lashes a shot that would beat most goalkeepers but Ricardo is an agile fellow and tips it wide. Great save!

21 mins – The corner causes mayhem but Owen and Andy Cole between them can't get a shot away and Ricardo fists it clear.

25 mins – Portugal's turn to threaten but Figo's free kick is glanced wide by Nuno Gomes.

30 mins – Luis Boa Morte is a nuisance. Edgar does well to get to the byline, and he pulls it back to the

scorer of the opening goal who looks destined to get his second, but Richard Wright turns it away, before snaffling the rebound before anybody else.

33 mins – **YELLOW CARD**
Paul Scholes still can't tackle. He's in the book for a very late lunge on Rui Costa. England getting increasingly ragged.

36 mins – Andy Cole puts in his contender for 'worst header of the tournament' by planting a diving header about 10 yards wide of Ricardo's goal. It was a good ball from Scholes but an awful finish.

38 mins – **YELLOW CARD**
Paulo Sousa is the first Portugal player in the book, he is late into a tackle on Ashley Cole and is carded without a fuss.

43 mins – Frank Lampard goes probing and he feeds a nice ball into Ashley Cole, but his low drive is just wide. It's either a concern or a very good tactic that Ashley Cole is having all of England's chances.

45 mins – Two added minutes here

45+1 mins – How have England not scored here? Firstly Joe Cole flashes a cross in that Michael

Owen is alive to, his header is pushed wide by Ricardo for a corner. Beckham's delivery is right on the money and Rio Ferdinand leaps highest but Ricardo is there again, tipping it over the bar for a third corner. Fernando Couto heads this one away but it is retrieved by Sol Campbell of all people, but he shows a calm head to find Scholes on the edge of the box. His shot is hit well but Ricardo saves and holds and that'll be that for the half.

HALF TIME: Portugal 1 – 0 England

It took England a while to get going and by the time they did it was too late. England have had more than enough chances to be level but have found Ricardo in great form. Portugal have only managed 3 shots to England's 8 but they are ahead on the only statistic that matters.

KICK OFF – Portugal get us back underway.

49 mins – Portugal are defending in huge numbers. Nuno Gomes is ploughing a lone furrow up front at the moment.

54 mins – Joe Cole is trying to unlock the door. He commits a couple of defenders and squeezes a pass to Beckham, but his shot is wide under severe pressure.

58 mins – Free kick outside the box for England, in Beckham territory. Hits the wall.

61 mins – **Substitution for Portugal**. A double change as Helder and Sergio Conceicao replace Edgar and Rui Costa. Helder is a holding midfielder which perhaps gives an indication of where Portugal's intentions lie.

65 mins – There's activity on the England bench as they go searching an equaliser.

67 mins – **Substitution for England.** Paul Scholes has had a poor game by his high standards; he's replaced by Kieron Dyer, whilst Emile Heskey is on for the ineffective Andy Cole.

69 mins – Almost an instant impact from a substitute, Heskey outmuscles Litos to get on the end of a Joe Cole cross but he heads over the bar.

72 mins – Off the post! England over commit and when their attack breaks down, it's Sergio Conceicao who is striding towards England's box. His low shot is well hit but it strikes the outside of the post and goes behind. England still have hope.

74 mins – Dangerous free kick for Portugal but Figo can also only hit the wall. Last 15 already.

78 mins – Post again! Nuno Gomes this time, who beats Ashley Cole with a lovely piece of skill but curls his effort onto the post and it flies away for a throw in. England hanging on by a thread.

81 mins – **Substitution for England.** Last throw of the dice as Steven Gerrard is on for Frank Lampard

82 mins – England his the crossbar! David Beckham takes responsibility from the edge of the box, his effort beats Ricardo but cannons back off the crossbar. Joe Cole helps the rebound back into the box but Heskey can't make the most of it.

84 mins – Chance for the newly arrived Gerrard but his shot is wide of the far post. England having a late rally but still can't find a goal.

88 mins – Ashley Cole pumps a free kick into the box and Gerrard knocks it down for Beckham, but his first time shot is wide of the post.

89 mins – **YELLOW CARD**

Joe Cole is booked for complaining about time wasting. This wastes times. Portugal enjoying it.

90 mins – **YELLOW CARD**

Nuno Gomes gets away from Rio Ferdinand who pulls him back. Needs must, but Portugal have the ball where they want it. Three added minutes.

FULL TIME: Portugal 1 – 0 England

Oh dear. England comfortably had the better of the game but couldn't beat Ricardo, though Portugal's centre backs were also excellent. Whilst you'd still back England to get out of the group, they almost certainly won't be winning it now.

Whilst we lick our wounds, the tournament continues. Russia and Costa Rica ends in a 2-2 draw, though Costa Rica will be furious at relinquishing a two goal lead. France's 2-0 win over Paraguay eliminates the South Americans, gone just 6 days into the tournament with a game to spare. Russia will fancy their chances of beating them in the final game, and if France and Costa Rica draw we'll have three teams on 5 points and the calculators come out.

Japan are out the very next day, their big party ended emphatically by a 4-1 defeat to Turkey. Japan had the nerve to take the lead but Turkey equalised on the stroke of half time and it was all downhill from there. South Africa are also eliminated, the Czech's look a good outside bet and they win 3-1 here to secure their place in the last 16.

South Korea hold Spain to 0-0 for 74 minutes but Fernando Morientes breaks the deadlock and their host nation spirit as it finishes 3-0. Mexico edge past Belgium 1-0 which puts Spain through and means South Korea can join them if they can defeat Mexico in the final game. Belgium need to beat Spain and hope the other result goes their way, this also has the potential to get complicated. South Korea were real life semi-finalists though nobody is really sure how, they had some decisions go their way that others disagreed with. And by disagreed with, I mean were proven to be horrendously inaccurate by TV replays. Still, the record shows they finished 4th, which is an achievement.

Imagine making your International debut in the World Cup finals, climbing off the bench on 62 minutes and scoring twice including a last minute winner. You are Haruna Babangida, inspiring Nigeria's 2-1 win over Austria in group D. That, coupled with Brazil's 4-0 win over India, puts the Super Eagles in the last 16 along with Brazil, though they will play off in the final game to see who tops the group.

Damien Duff secures a late draw for Ireland against the USA after Joe Max Moore of Everton had given the Americans the early advantage. Argentina need a late Roberto Ayala header to see off Poland and qualify with a game to spare, a result which also means Ireland can join them with a win over Poland. USA can also still qualify if they beat Argentina and Poland don't win.

Group H is out of sync again and plays next. Yugoslavia earn a 1-1 draw with Senegal, a result that suits Germany. In a strange turn of events, Ballack misses a penalty and Didi Hamann is sent off but Germany defeat Uruguay 1-0 thanks to Fredi Bobic. It puts Germany top of the group but all four teams can still qualify.

Portugal defeat Tunisia 2-0, Nuno Gomes grabbing both goals. That's probably the best result for us, I'll take just getting through at this stage and if Tunisia were on 6 points we'd be in trouble. But instead we head to the Chamsil Olympic Stadium in Seoul needing a win against Ecuador to restore some confidence…

England vs Ecuador – World Cup Group F

To some English fans, Ecuador is just a popular trance song from the 90s, but right now they have a pretty big chance of eliminating England in the group stage and making my mission to get the best out of the golden generation a complete and utter failure. With that in mind, changes are afoot.

I've spent the week grovelling to Steven Gerrard, I should never have dropped him. He's back at Lampard's expense. I've also gone for Kieron Dyer over Paul Scholes, a ludicrous sentence but when you rely on a team to dribble and overrun your opponents, we don't really get the best out of Scholesy. Otherwise though, we're unchanged.

England: Wright, G Neville, Campbell, Ferdinand, Ash. Cole, Gerrard, Beckham, J. Cole, Dyer, Owen, An. Cole. **Subs:** Kirkland, Carragher, Woodgate, Lampard, Scholes, Heskey, Fowler.

Ecuador can't be taken lightly. Their loss to Tunisia has given me hope that they maybe aren't as good as their 2014 counterparts, but they have a striker up front with 20 for finishing.

Ecuador: Astrada, Espinoza, Ayovi, I. Hurtado, Porozo, Sanchez, Aguinaga, Moreira, E. Hurtado, Kaviedes, Mora. **Subs:** Matamba, Ibarra, Montano, Reasco, Delgado, Blandon, Minda

With the anthems done and dusted, the players are ready. Somebody will make themselves a hero.

KICK OFF - England do the honours and get the game started.

4 mins – England haven't been able to assert any dominance on the match so far, Ecuador have settled much the better.

8 mins – Great save from Richard Wright! Sanchez meets Aguinaga's cross with a sweet right foot shot but Wright reacts like a cat to push it away.

11 mins – Typical of England's start, Joe Cole spins in a lovely cross but there's nobody anywhere near it. They are very disjointed in their attacking display so far.

13 mins – **GOAL FOR ECUADOR! England 0 – 1 Ecuador (Eduardo Hurtado)**

UH OH. A frighteningly simple goal, a throw in finds Moreira who slides in Aguinaga on the right side of the penalty area. The winger looks up and squares the ball for the arriving Eduardo Hurtado who has a tap in from all of four yards. England in trouble now.

16 mins – **RED CARD (Geovanny Espinoza)**

Is this the lifeline England need? Beckham's free kick is cleared but when the ball is recycled, Dyer slips Gerrard in behind a defence that is still coming out from the free kick. Espinoza panics and scythes down Gerrard, which referee Tarmo Sirel deems to be a professional foul. He's probably right, even if Gerrard is a yard out of the penalty area nobody was going to catch him legally.

17 mins – **Substitution for Ecuador**. Kaviedes is hooked for Andres Minda, a centre half was always going to come on. Beckham's free kick hits the wall.

19 mins – **YELLOW CARD**

Eduardo Hurtado is booked for a blatant trip on Ashley Cole. Ecuador are rattled.

20 mins – Beckham delivers the free kick and Andy Cole gets the glancing header on it but Astrada parries it away for a corner. The corner comes to nothing.

25 mins – Ecuador have retreated to a back 9, there's barely even an outlet. They are able to contain England with worrying ease though.

30 mins – Nothing happening I'm afraid.

35 mins – Seriously, somebody do something. Please.

41 mins – **GOAL FOR ENGLAND! England 1 – 1 Ecuador (Joe Cole)**

JC is the saviour! A well worked goal for England, playing against pretty much a back 9, as Dyer finds Joe Cole who weaves one way and then the other before angling a shot across the keeper and in off the far post. England's first goal of the tournament has come at a time where they looked at their lowest ebb: struggling to break down 10 man Ecuador.

HALF TIME: England 1 – 1 Ecuador

England were in trouble but the red card has changed the dynamics. Can England find a way to breakdown this stubborn Ecuador side for a second time? They'll also have to be wary of Ecuador's pace on the break, but they desperately need to start making some chances.

KICK OFF – Ecuador get us back underway

47 mins – **Substitution for Ecuador**. Could they not have done this at half time? Blandon is on for Sanchez. On we go.

50 mins – Joe and Andy combine, but Andy Cole's volley is wayward. It's fair to say he has done little

to improve his International reputation in the two games so far.

53 mins – Another chance, this time Kieron Dyer is denied by Astrada after good work from Steven Gerrard. Dyer hit his shot powerfully towards the top corner but Astrada was equal to it before his defence helped him out and completed the clearance.

56 mins – Off the post! Gerrard takes the ball on the burst and hits a low shot that beats the keeper but not the post. It's got to happen for England sooner or later you'd think.

60 mins – Gerrard is a growing influence here. David Beckham's cross is blocked but Gerrard picks up the loose ball, and another low shot is spilled by Astrada before he pounces on the loose ball.

63 mins – Gary Neville and Beckham combine down the right, Beckham's low cross is controlled by Owen but in turning away from his marker, it gives Astrada half a chance to smother the loose ball which he does.

65 mins – **YELLOW CARD**

Jose Mora goes in the book for a late challenge on Joe Cole. Any Mora that and he'll be off. This is no time for jokes.

70 mins – Ayovi goes on a gutst run for Ecuador, beating 3 England players but his cross is cleared by Ashley Cole.

74 mins – England get sloppy in possession and concede a free kick out on the right. Ayovi whips it in and Moreira gets his head to the ball and forces Wright to tip it over. He then punches the corner away before shouting at anybody who will listen. His team need to up it again.

78 mins – **Substitutions for England**. Gary Neville jogs off, with Frank Lampard on. It looks like Gerrard is going to right back. Robbie Fowler is on for Andy Cole, in a like for like swap of strikers who have never really mimicked their club form at International level.

80 mins – Astrada saves again! This time it's Kieron Dyer, who is fed by Beckham on the edge of the box but his shot is too close to Astrada who again opts to parry.

81 mins – The resulting throw in ends with Joe Cole crossing for Owen, who is tackled but the loose ball runs for Beckham. His low shot looks for

all the world like a goal but that man Astrada is there to get fingertips on it. The corner is headed away.

84 mins – Another corner, but this time Frank Lampard gets his head to it and guess what? Astrada saves again.

88 mins – Crossbar! Joe and Ashley combine down the left, Joe crosses for former West Ham teammate Lampard and his half volley beats Astrada but hits the crossbar. Time is running out...

89 mins – **Substitution for England.** Rio Ferdinand is off, Emile Heskey is on. Three up front, Sol Campbell at the back. It's desperation time.

90 mins – **GOAL FOR ENGLAND! England 2 – 1 Ecuador (Frank Lampard)**

They thought it was all over but it's only just begun! England finally get their reward for banging on the Ecuador door (Ecuadoor?) for the majority of the last hour with Frank Lampard absolutely bludgeoning this into the net. It was probably the only way this pesky goalkeeper would be beaten for a second time and, after hitting the crossbar just moments ago, Lampard is now buried beneath about 25 men in England kit or tracksuits. Get in!

90+2 mins – Ecuador swing a cross in from the right which is claimed by Richard Wright. He collapses to the floor to waste time. We all feel like doing that, Richard. Incidentally, England have put Gerrard at centre half with Campbell and Kieron Dyer at right back to try and keep some sort of shape for the remaining time.

FULL TIME: England 2 – 1 Ecuador

About as far from convincing as you can get but England have won a match and are remarkably now second in the group. Tunisia will be an interesting clash in 4 days' time. This was minutes away from being a disaster, but questions will be raised about how far England can actually go after an eternal struggle like this against 10 man Ecuador.

If you think England will be getting bad press back home, the Italians are waiting at the airport with rotten tomatoes again. In one of the great World Cup shocks, China defeat Italy 1-0, making my prediction about Italy a mere few pages ago seem like utter rubbish. Incredibly, China managed 0 shots to Italy's 12 – the goal coming from the head of Fabio Cannavaro in a freak incident just before half time. Cameroon play out their second successive 2-2 draw, this time with Denmark, which leaves China top of the group and Denmark bottom, though again all four teams can still make it through.

As we're now at the final group games we've reached the point where the group matches are played simultaneously. This can only be good news from a reporting point of view. Holders France take part in one of the most entertaining games in World Cup history, defeating Costa Rica 5-3 having trailed 1-0, been pegged back from 3-3 before finally romping home. That defeat leaves the door ajar for Russia to qualify, but a 1-0 defeat to already eliminated Paraguay means they end up with the wooden spoon in Group A, and Costa Rica go through after all.

Group B was already settled but the coveted top spot was up for grabs, which means avoiding France in the last 16. Czech Republic nabbed a 1-0 win though Turkey had the better of the game between what looks like two quite evenly matched sides. Japan beat South Africa in the dead rubber, saving Japan some face in their home tournament. France vs Turkey could be a good game.

Spain top group C with a 100% record, defeating Belgium 2-1 to breeze through. They are joined by Mexico, who score a late equaliser against South Korea to deny the co-hosts a place in the last 16. Before this tournament, no hosts had gone out in the group stage, and we've now lost two in two days.

Group D had the shootout between Nigeria and Brazil, where the losers will face Spain in the next round. Brazil ease to a 2-0 win but lose goalscorer Amoroso for the remainder of the tournament. India score their first goal of the tournament but ship another 4 in a 4-1 loss to Austria. With 13 goals conceded, India are very worthy of the wooden spoon.

We wave goodbye to Ireland, a disappointing 1-0 defeat to Poland ends Mick McCarthy's side's stay in the tournament. Roy Keane played every match, in stark contrast to his sharp exit from Ireland's pre-tournament training camp in reality. Poland's win sees them advance along with Argentina, who wrap up the 100% record with a 3-2 win over USA. Argentina actually finished the match with Batistuta in goal as Cavallero was sent off on 74 minutes with the score at 3-1. Clint Mathis converted the penalty but the USA couldn't test Batistuta's reflexes. The runner up in England's group will face the Argentines in the last 16.

And so, to Group F we go…

Tunisia vs England – World Cup Group F

A draw will be enough for England to advance but my word, they need a performance here. Tunisia were England's opponents in their opening game of World Cup 98 and Shearer and Scholes saw them off that day, but what now for this crop of players?

England have made changes. Lampard is back in the starting 11 after his matching winning contribution from the bench against Ecuador. Phil is in for Gary at right back, and Paul Scholes is restored but as a striker in place on Andy Cole. My theory here is that Cole, Heskey and Fowler have been ineffectual so let's try somebody who is technically brilliant to see if he can at least link the play.

England: Wright, P Neville, Ash. Cole, Campbell, Ferdinand, Lampard, Beckham, J. Cole, Dyer, Scholes, Owen. **Subs:** Kirkland, Carragher, Woodgate, Gerrard, An. Cole, Heskey, Fowler

Tunisia: El Ouaer, Mkacher, Trabelsi, Nouira, Chouhcane, M'Hadhebi, Gabsi, Bouazizi, Godhbane, Sellimi, Baya. **Subs:** Ben Slimane, Zitouni, Jelassi, Essidiri, Senoussi, Bouzaiene, Jaziri.

Both sets of fans appreciate the national anthems, and it's time to get this crucial game underway.

KICK OFF – Michael Owen and Paul Scholes get us started.

4 mins – Early chance for Paul Scholes in his more advanced position. Ashley Cole, who is proving quite the outlet down the left during this tournament, sends in a tempting cross that Scholes meets with a firm header but El Ouaer is equal to it, pushing the ball away and his defensive colleagues complete the clearance.

6 mins – Tunisia threaten now as Sellimi curls in a neat free kick but Ashley Cole gets a good block on a shot from Nouira to divert the danger.

10 mins – If England thought Tunisia would be a pushover, they are very much mistaken. A spell of possession ends with Bouazizi bending one over the bar from distance. A poor finish to a nice move.

13 mins – **YELLOW CARD**

The yellow card is out and it's a big one. Rio Ferdinand is booked for an innocuous trip on Sellimi. That will put him out of the last 16 clash with Argentina, if England get there.

15 mins – Bouazizi again! Much more of a chance this, as he half-volleys over from the edge of the box. England living dangerously.

19 mins – Better for England, as Beckham's cross finds Owen, who spins his marker and hits a shot that the keeper spills. It's cleared before anyone in England white can pounce on the loose ball though

24 mins – The pace has relented here, unlike the rain. It's lashing down here in Daegu.

27 mins – Sustained possession for England results in Beckham finding Owen, but again his shot is saved. The ball is recycled and this time Lampard finds Owen, but El Ouaer pushes it behind. This is getting silly. Scholes has a shot from the corner but it's deflected behind before Tunisia eventually clear.

29 mins – **GOAL FOR ENGLAND! Tunisia 0 – 1 England (Ashley Cole)**

It had been coming. England are piling men forward and nothing proves that point more than Ashley Cole getting on the end of David Beckham's cross to put England ahead. It's more or less a far post tap-in in the end, with England's pressure finally telling.

34 mins – England have their tails up now, popping the ball about confidently before Beckham tries to find Lampard's run but the goalkeeper is out to make a smart interception.

37 mins – **GOAL FOR ENGLAND! Tunisia 0 – 2 England (Kieron Dyer)**

That's more like it! England finding their stride now, as Joe Cole slips a through ball for Kieron Dyer to run onto. Dyer rounds the keeper and converts into an empty net and England are cruising towards that clash with Argentina.

38 mins – Incidentally, Portugal lead in Seoul against Ecuador. Fernando Couto has scored with a header from a corner.

42 mins – 2-0 to Portugal, Joao Tomas with the headed goal. England are definitely playing for second place.

HALF TIME: Tunisia 0 – 2 England

Excellent half for England with a two-goal cushion to show for their efforts. Nothing daft now and they'll be in the last 16.

KICK OFF – Tunisia get the second half started.

49 mins – This is a terrible effort, but I suppose you have to give him points for effort. Paul Scholes chips a cross over and Kieron Dyer decides a bicycle kick is the way forward. Predictably, it is nowhere near the goal.

53 mins – Good hands from Richard Wright, Baya rifles in a good effort that the England stopper does well to save. It's still soaking out there.

57 mins – **Substitution for Tunisia**. Essidiri is on for Bouazizi whilst Senoussi is on for Godhbane.

61 mins – Tunisia are going for it after those substitutions, new arrival Essidiri has a header at goal which Wright just about keeps out before Phil Neville is calmness personified to pass the ball clear.

63 mins – David Beckham's turn to have a crack, his effort from distance skims off the surface an Al Ouaer pushes it away. The Tunisia goalkeeper has earned his keep today.

65 mins – **GOAL FOR ENGLAND! Tunisia 0 – 3 England (Michael Owen)**

Cherry, meet cake. England's key man is finally off the mark for this tournament, dropping a shoulder as he races past Chouhcane and finishing confidently past the keeper. Surely that is that.

66 mins – **YELLOW CARD**

Tunisia are beaten and perhaps a little frustrated. Sellimi goes in the book for an elbow in Rio Ferdinand's back as they jump for a header.

68 mins – **Substitution for England**. England take the chance to rest some players with Argentina in their sights. Captain Beckahm is off for Steven Gerrard, whilst Owen is replaced by Liverpool colleague Emile Heskey. Sol Campbell takes the armband.

72 mins – Paul Scholes has an effort saved by the keeper. He's made a huge difference playing further forward.

77 mins – Everybody wants a goal now. Joe Cole tries from about 40 yards, but it's well wide.

80 mins – **Substitution for England.** Kieron Dyer is off to be replaced by Andy Cole. Dyer's stock has certainly risen as the tournament has progressed.

82 mins – **Substitution for Tunisia**. Tunisia replace M'Hadhebi with Bouzaiene.

85 mins – The England fans are singing "If Heskey scores, we're on the pitch!" We nearly have a crowd scene as he meets Phil Neville's cross with a bullet header but El Ouaer saves.

88 mins – Sol Campbell gets a header all wrong from a Joe Cole corner, it flies well over the bar. Time is ticking down now.

90 mins – Just two added minutes, even the officials know the game is up

90+1 mins – Paul Scholes deserves a goal for his performance today but El Ouaer makes yet another save to keep it at 3-0. That'll be about it.

FULL TIME: Tunisia 0 – 3 England

Job done for England, crisis has been averted and it will be a re-match with Argentina in the last 16. Joe Cole is awarded man of the match and a perfect 10 rating but any of the front 6 could have claimed man of the match.

With Portugal beating Ecuador, we'll have to settle for second place and a clash with Argentina but I'm just happy to come back with two wins after that rocky start. Rio Ferdinand will miss the last 16 tie through suspension, but Argentina will at least be missing their first choice goalkeeper.

China advance! They draw 1-1 with Denmark to go through at the expense of their opponents but also Cameroon, who are comfortably beaten 3-0 by Italy. Italy top the group despite that little hiccup against China.

In the final group, Germany right some wrongs as Ballack scores a pen this time in a 2-0 win over Senegal. Uruguay take second spot after a late winner against Yugoslavia. It means we'll have Germany vs China and Italy vs Uruguay to look forward to.

The very eagle eyed among you, you will note that in the actual 2002 World Cup the last 16 draw didn't follow the traditional "Winner of Group A plays runner of Group B" format whereas the game has reverted to this. The reason the real tournament had a different approach was to keep the co-hosts playing in their own country as the top half of the last 16 draw was scheduled in South Korean stadiums, with the bottom half in Japan. So for example, under the "normal" format South Korea as winners of Group D would have played their last 16 clash in Japan. All of this is academic though as it is fairly pedantic for a computer game to need to consider logistics, and you might question why I've brought it up at all.

With that, holders France get the last 16 underway by defeating Turkey 1-0. Stephane Dalmat of Inter Milan (and briefly Tottenham Hotspur in the future) gets the goal 20 minutes from time but Turkey didn't manage a single shot on target and were lucky to get away lightly.

Brazil are also through to set up a repeat of the 1998 final, two goals from Elber guides them past Mexico. Elber has just secured a £19m move to Real Madrid, so his stock is very high at the moment. He and Ronaldo have the potential to be a devastating partnership and will take some stopping.

Fan Zhiyi has been a CM favourite for years, and by 01/02 he is a defender, midfielder or forward playing for Crystal Palace. Versatility seems to be key as he rams home a 77th minute equaliser for China against Germany and would you believe it, the match goes to extra time. Those mean old Germans score in the 105th minute though to win on the Golden Goal rule. Golden Goal was a rule brought in whereby the first goal scored in extra time would be the winner. Germany profited from it in the Euro 96 final with Oliver Bierhoff getting the decisive goal, but here it's his replacement and World Cup expert Miroslav Klose who nabs the winner and breaks Chinese hearts. They've had an incredible run though.

Now though, it's England's turn...

Argentina vs England – World Cup Last 16

Do you remember watching David Beckham flick a leg at Diego Simeone? How he barely made contact and Simeone went down like he had been shot? Beckham saw red and so did I. Simeone had angered 10 year old me.

Do you remember 1986? I don't, I had the obvious handicap of not being born, but if you lived through that World Cup you'll know the resentment you felt towards Diego Maradona for leaping and punching the ball into the net. Peter Shilton was mad. You don't make Peter Shilton mad and get away with it. Except Maradona then went one better and skinned the entire team to put Argentina through to the semi-finals. "The hand of a rascal" Bobby Robson called it. I'd use a different word to rascal.

David Beckham would get his revenge in the 2002 World Cup. Michael Owen went down under the slightest breeze and Beckham completed his recovery from people burning effigy's of him to being nicknamed Goldenballs. It was an awful penalty, smashed down the middle of the goal about a yard to the right of the keeper who seemed to get stuck. Maybe he was in awe of Goldenballs. Or maybe it was just the football world putting itself right.

That was a group game, but this is straight knockout. Failure is not an option. I'm sticking with the same team that beat Tunisia, where possible. Rio Ferdinand is banned, so Jonny Woodgate is in. He's a big game player. Steve McManaman is ruled out for the remainder of the tournament with a calf strain, but he wasn't in the 11 anyway.

England: Wright, Campbell, Woodgate, P Neville, Ash. Cole, Lampard, Beckham, J Cole, Dyer, Scholes, Owen. **Subs:** Kirkland, Carragher, Southagte, Gerrard, An. Cole, Heskey, Fowler.

Argentina manager Marcelo Bielsa has only goals on his mind. It's 3-5-2 but Ortega is the right wing back with Zanetti in central midfield. He's either mad or a genius. They're just really good all round. Carlos Roa is recalled in goal for the suspended Cavallero – Roa saved two penalties in the shootout in 1998.

Argentina: Roa, Ayala, Samuel, Berizzo, Navas, Ortega, Zanetti, Almeyda, Veron, Saviola, Batistuta.

Subs: Gonzalez, Franco, Solari, Chamot, Palermo, Rotchen, Coloccini.

It's always a feisty affair between these two countries so the pre-match crowd hasn't been as friendly as some of the other fixtures. Let's get to the game

KICK OFF – Argentina get us underway here in Kobe.

4 mins – It's been a good start from both teams, you have to say it's incredibly open. You'd probably expect as much with Ortega at right wing back.

8 mins – **GOAL FOR ENGLAND! Argentina 0 – 1 England (Ashley Cole)**

Ashley Cole got no goals for Arsenal last season but this is his second goal of this World Cup alone. We talked about Ortega playing right wing back in the build-up and the problem with that is clear to see here. Cole is not tracked by anybody as he receives a pass from Joe Cole on the edge of the box, driving into the box and shooting low across Roa who has no chance. England lead!

11 mins – There's euphoria in the England end still, 80 more minutes to get through yet though.

14 mins – **PENALTY TO ENGLAND**
Dyer bursts into the area and shimmies past Roa who has come flying out. The Mallorca goalkeeper brings him down – it's as clear a penalty as you will ever see…

15 mins – **RED CARD (Carlos Roa, Argentina)**

The old professional foul, denying a goal scoring opportunity. Call it what you want, it's a red card offence. Argentina need a new penalty saving hero.

Substitution for Argentina. Leo Franco is on for Javier Saviola, this is of course Argentina's last available goalkeeper.

16 mins - **GOAL FOR ENGLAND! Argentina 0 – 2 England (Ashley Cole)**

Er, I really must remember to set a penalty taker. Ashley Cole sends Leo France the wrong way, he's got three for the tournament now. Golden boot?
19 mins – Argentina are trying to reorganise. Ortega isn't at right wing back now, needless to say.

22 mins – What an effort this is. Almeyda takes an innocuous looking throw in to Batistuta, who dummies and lets the ball run across his body before unleashing a swerving, dipping half volley

that looks destined to be one of the great World Cup goals, but Richard Wright somehow gets fignertips to it. What an effort, what a save.

27 mins – England are happy to stick with what they have. The onus is on Argentina now.

32 mins – A glimmer for Argentina as Ortega delivers a great dead ball into the England 6 yard box but Walter Samuel can only head straight up in the air and over the bar.

38 mins – **YELLOW CARD**

Huge cheers from the Argentina fans as David Beckham goes in the book for a trip on Almeyda. A little bit needless

44 mins – One added minute. England not going anywhere in a hurry.

HALF TIME: Argentina 0 – 2 England

England 2-0 up and Argentina down to 10. This is not a dream. The quarter finals are beckoning. Once England got their goals they have managed the game perfectly.

KICK OFF – England restart the game

48 mins – That's a great save from Leo Franco to deny Beckham. Frank Lampard did all the hard work and got the better of Juan Veron before shifting the ball square for Beckham to strike, but it's pushed over the bar.

49 mins – Woodwork! Beckham's corner is on the money and Woodgate's header hits the crossbar flush before Argentina scramble it away. England close to sealing the deal there.

55 mins – **GOAL FOR ENGLAND! Argentina 0 – 3 England (Kieron Dyer)**

Simple goal this, Ashley Cole is at the heart of it as he travels 40 yards unopposed down the left and finds Paul Scholes in the D on the edge of the box. He pokes a pass through to Dyer, who finishes first time beyond Leo Franco. Easy for England now, and it's only Germany next.

60 mins – England have done their job professionally here. Keeping the ball and making Argentina do all the chasing. Argentina can't get on the ball to make any inroads. They want to go home.

67 mins – **YELLOW CARD**

We're always saying how it is funny that Paul Scholes can't tackle, here he is several hours late into a challenge with Zanetti. Simple booking.

72 mins – Substitution for England. With the game won, Michael Owen is withdrawn for Andy Cole. Joe Cole is also given a rest, with Steven Gerrard on.

75 mins – YELLOW CARD

Kieron Dyer knocks the ball past Walter Samuel, who knows he is beaten for pace and hands off Dyer. The big centre back gets a yellow card for his misdemeanour.

Substitution for Argentina. Gabriel Batistuta trudges off to be replaced by Martin Palermo. Batistuta is 33 and chasing the ball has understandably tired him.

77 mins – YELLOW CARD

Phil Neville is the latest to be booked, he fouls Ortega out on the touchline. These cards are a bit needless and carry on through the tournament.

81 mins – Substitution for Argentina. Roberto Ayala is off and Pablo Rotchen is on. That's like for like, and smacks of players just getting some pitch time.

83 mins – The game has resembled a friendly in recent minutes, nobody really even trying to score a goal.

86 mins – I take it back, Steven Gerrard is desperate to make his mark after coming on as a sub. He skins fellow substitute Rotchen but his fierce shot is parried by Leo Franco. Argentina just want the whistle.

89 mins – **YELLOW CARD**

Sol Campbell is the latest to go in the book. Discipline, lads. Campbell sells himself against Javier Zanetti and just hacks him down. Stupid. Veron smashes the free kick over the bar and into the crowd. Ironic cheers all round

FULL TIME: Argentina 0 – 3 England

Revenge for England! David Beckham captains the side to a handsome victory and exorcises the demons of 1998. The feel good factor is back! A last 8 clash with Germany awaits.

Spain are at it again. Just when you think they've shaken off their glorious failures tag, they lose 2-0 to Nigeria. Taribo West, another cover star, is man of the match. Garba Lawal of Roda scores both goals and you have to say that is a bigger shocker than England beating Argentina. Probably.

Nigeria will play Czech Republic in the last 8, the Czech's edging Costa Rica 1-0 thanks to Liverpool's Patrick Berger. The bottom half of the draw is looking a lot weaker than the top half, in my opinion.

Yep, definitely weaker. My tip Italy are beaten extra time by Uruguay. Vincenzo Montella scores an equaliser to force extra time but sub Federico Megallanes scores the golden goal winner. Italy managed 23 shots to Uruguay's 4, with 18 of those on target. Carini in the Uruguay goal gets press praise after the match. He is presumably some sort of octopus. Carini is actually on the books of Juventus but very much behind Buffon in the pecking order. Still, it'll be interesting to see if he is sacked by his club in the same way South Korea striker Ahn Jung-Hwan was cast aside by Perugia after he knocked Italy out of the real World Cup. Grown men made that decision.

Remember when Portugal beat me in the first match? Oh how we have grown since then.

Portugal though are the latest casualties from the bottom half of the draw, drawing 0-0 with Poland and going on to lose on penalties. Our scourge Boa Morte is sent off on 56 minutes for pushing Tomasz Waldoch over and you can't do that in any walk of life. 8 penalties each later and Helder misses the vital penalty. The bottom half of the draw now has Nigeria vs Czech Republic and Uruguay vs Poland. The top has France vs Brazil and Germany vs England. That hardly seems fair.

For reasons I don't understand, we're up first...

England vs Germany – World Cup Quarter Final

Gareth Southgate, the whole of England is with you. Oh it's saved...

We still believe. The problem with having two games against the same team about 25,000 words apart is that I've already covered the vast history between the two. However in more recent history, the two sides have traded blows in qualifying with a win apiece so far in each other's back yards. It is therefore perhaps fitting that the decider is being played in the neutral venue of Daegu, Korea. England have looked far better since moving Paul Scholes to a forward position to combine with Owen, Dyer and Joe Cole, so it's no surprise that the only change is Rio Ferdinand for Jonny

Woodgate.

England: Wright, P Neville, Ash. Cole, Ferdinand, Campbell, Lampard, Beckham, J. Cole, Dyer, Scholes, Owen. **Subs:** Kirkland, Carragher, Southgate, Gerrard, Cole, Heskey, Fowler

Germany still play 3-4-1-2 with Scholl as the playmaker behind the front two. They are without Christian Ziege and Sebastien Deisler though, both are injured and out for the tournament.

Germany: Kahn, Linke, Worns, Nowotny, Heinrich, Bode, Hamann, Ballack, Scholl, Bobic, Neuville. **Subs:** Asamoah, Rost, Baumann, Rehmer, Klose, Jancker, Kehl

Incidentally, Campbell, Phil Neville, Beckham and Scholes are one yellow away from a ban. Germany have Thomas Linke and Oliver Neuville in the same boat.

It's 30 degrees in Daegu, the hottest temperature England have played in so far. Will that be a factor?

KICK OFF – Germany kick the match off.

5 mins – First sniff of goal is from England, Ashley "the danger man" Cole goes on his now trademark run down the left and whips the ball over but

Oliver Kahn gathers with England players waiting. Good hands.

8 mins – Good spot from the referee, Lampard has his shirt pulled by Linke and it's a free kick about 25 yards from goal. Beckham pings a trademark effort up and over the wall but Kahn is equal to it. The big stopper looks in good form today.

11 mins – Germany's turn to work the goalkeeper, this time Oliver Neuville shows great control and gets a snapshot away. Wright is down well to push it away and Ashley Cole completes the clearance.

13 mins – Germany are turning the screw now. Neuville and Bobic combine, Bobic outmuscles Campbell but Wright is equal to his low drive at the cost of a corner. Campbell atones by heading it away.

17 mins – Joe Cole tries to restore some authority for England but his effort from 30 yards is speculative at best, and goes well over the bar.

20 mins – Ashley Cole is off and running down the left again and this time he spots Frank Lampard arriving on the edge of the box. Lampard meets it with a side foot volley but it is a yard over the bar.

25 mins – More England pressure, as Beckham finds Owen but his volley is high and wide. England have wrestled back control.

31 mins – Linke is again penalised for holding, this time Paul Scholes, but there's no card. A clever free kick routine sees Ashley Cole, Lampard and Joe Cole combine and ends with the West Ham man forcing a save from Kahn. The ball spills to Beckham, on the penalty spot with the goal gaping, but he slips as he hits it and it goes wide. Beckham looks at the turf, we've all done it. Just not in a World Cup quarter final.

35 mins – Fierce tempo to this game, it's a bit of a basketball match at times. Neuville cuts inside on the corner of the box, but his low shot is saved by Richard Wright.

40 mins – **GOAL FOR ENGLAND! England 1 – 0 Germany (Frank Lampard)**

Breakthrough! It's brilliant from Frank Lampard, who gets the better of Michael Ballack before shooting low through bodies and it nestles in the bottom corner. Kahn had no chance with it coming through bodies like that. England are ahead!

43 mins – Chance for Germany to level it up but Fredi Bobic loses compsure and fire well over the bar from inside the area. A bit of a let off.

45 mins – **YELLOW CARD**

Thomas Linke is finally booked, this time for tripping Paul Scholes. You can't do that to Paul Scholes.

45+1 mins – **GOAL FOR ENGLAND! England 2 – 0 Germany (David Beckham)**

The resulting free kick is an absolute peach. Up and over the wall from Beckham and it finds the top corner. I don't believe it. What a time to get a second goal.

HALF TIME: England 2 – 0 Germany

Wow, England are running into form at just the right time. Taking out Argentina and Germany in consecutive rounds would be incredible, and a real show of intent. But there's still time for Germany's tournament gene to kick in.

KICK OFF – England get us restarted here in Daegu.

47 mins – Germany have had the hair dryer treatment, although I suppose that translates as Mr Dryer in Germany. What did I say about this being no time for jokes? Neuville is denied by Richard Wright again although this is a much more routine save.

48 mins – Wright is beaten this time but saved by the crossbar! It's still shaking now, as Marco Bode meets Neuville's cross with a thunderous volley that nearly breaks the goal frame. A let off for England.

51 mins – Owen threatens on the counter attack but his shot drifts harmlessly wide. It was a good run from Kieron Dyer to set up the chance but the angle was against Owen.

53 mins – **GOAL FOR ENGLAND! England 3 – 0 Germany (Frank Lampard)**

Lampard at it again! The Chelsea man has really vindicated his selection in the side and after initially being denied by Oliver Kahn, he follows in his own shot and taps in the rebound. Excellent play from England, who will surely now progress to the semi-finals.

54 mins – **YELLOW CARD**

Joe Cole is in the book, it's a proper scythe down to stop Ballack going any further. A dangerous free kick to defend now.

55 mins – GOAL FOR GERMANY! England 3 – 1 Germany (Michael Ballack)

Instant response from Germany, as Neuville's free kick bounces in front of Wright and he spills it straight to Michael Ballack who makes no mistake. That makes it interesting.

59 mins – GOAL FOR GERMANY! England 3 – 2 Germany (Fredi Bobic)

The more you anger Germany, the better they are. Moments after Richard Wright denies Neuville again, England switch off from the throw in. Ballack's cross finds Neuville, and although he is brilliantly denied by Rio Ferdinand, the loose ball falls to Bobic who lashes into the roof of the net. Game well and truly on.

61 mins – GOAL FOR GERMANY! England 3 – 3 Germany (Fredi Bobic)
Germany have a spring in their step now and England are a nervous wreck. Bobic takes on Sol Campbell, leaves the Arsenal man on his backside and smashes the ball in off the far post. Richard Wright looks crestfallen. England have conceded

three in 6 minutes and now the momentum is all with Germany.

63 mins – Kieron Dyer tries to give England some impetus, out running Didi Hamann before curling an effort towards goal which Kahn saves but spills. Christian Worns is on hand to help his captain out .

66 mins – This game has had everything and very nearly has a Phil Neville goal, but his low shot is inches wide. That would have been too much.

68 mins – Germany's turn to attack, as Ballack leads England a merry dance before forcing Wright to turn his shot behind. Scholl's corner is on the money and Nowotny meets it but Wright saves and Ferdinand hacks away.

70 mins – David Beckham tries a shot from about 30 yards but it's straight at Kahn. Big 20 minutes coming up.

74 mins – **Substitution for England.** England opt for some steel, introducing Gerrard for Joe Cole.

75 mins – **Substitution for Germany.** Germany have the opposite game plan, bringing on Miroslav Klose for Hamann.

80 mins – Phil, Phil will tear you apart. Well, he won't, but he has another shot that is so close to going in the England bench all jump up. It brushes the post. Still 3-3.

84 mins – Dyer finds Lampard in the box who gets his shot away but Kahn saves low down. He holds onto the ball and gives a wry smile.

90 mins – Both teams have rather settled for extra time, that 30 degree heat is starting to take effect.

FULL TIME: England 3 – 3 Germany (Match goes to Extra Time)

England have blown a 3-0 lead but have half an hour to save their blushes. Having said that, to lead Germany 3-0 in the first place is quite remarkable. A reminder that as soon as either team scores, the game is over. Otherwise, it will be a penalty shootout.

KICK OFF – Germany get extra time underway. Does either team have enough left to win this?

93 mins – Kieron Dyer has endless energy but long range shooting is not his speciality, it's not the best struck shot in the world and Kahn gathers it easily.

97 mins – Beckham delivers a free kick which Gerrard heads goalwards but it is blocked on the 6 yard line by Miroslav Klose. The corner is easily dealt with.

101 mins – Germany threaten from distance now, Jorg Heinrich has had a quiet game and his shot here is nowhere near making it 4-3.

HALF TIME IN EXTRA TIME: England 3 – 3 Germany

Anybody have that familiar sinking feeling? We know how a penalty shootout will play out.

KICK OFF – England get the last 15 minutes underway.

108 mins – Fredi Bobic is down injured but he is desperate to stay on. He waves away the physio. You have to applaud passion like that, provided he can still move.

110 mins – Neuville shoots from a ridiculous angle on the volley, it flies over the bar. Both sides are running out of energy and ideas.

116 mins – Bobic is still moving ok, but his shooting is wayward here. Scholl finds him about

25 yards out, but his curling effort is a tired one that drifts well wide.

120 mins – England, sensing the inevitably of a penalty shootout defeat, have one last throw of the dice. Germany flock around David Beckham on the edge of the box and the captain manages to nudge the ball to his right, where Kieron Dyer takes a touch before firing a low shot wide. The referee has his whistle in his mouth…

FULL TIME: England 3 – 3 Germany

MATCH GOES TO PENALTIES

I can't tell you how little I wanted to go to penalties with the Germans. I try to bring on Robbie Fowler for Phil Neville but you can't do that. Should have thought of that sooner really. Anyway, England have enough cool heads on the pitch to win this, sadly Germany have enough Germans on the pitch to win this. Let's see what happens.

Beckham SAVED (England 0 – 0 Germany)

Oh, this is not a good start. Beckham's penalty isn't bad but Kahn guess correctly and claws it away. First blood to Germany, and they haven't even taken yet.

Scholl SCORES (England 0 – 1 Germany)

Easy for Mehmet Scholl, he sends Richard Wright the wrong way.

Lampard SCORES (England 1 – 1 Germany)

Good pen, low and hard and Kahn goes the wrong way anyway. England on the board

Neuville MISSES (England 1 – 1 Germany)

What an awful penalty. Neuville steps up right footed and blazes it over the bar. Think Chris Waddle in 1990 but on his right. Neuville was born in Switzerland, which goes some way to explaining why his inherent penalty gene has failed here.

Owen SCORES (England 2 – 1 Germany)

Smashed down the middle of the goal, Kahn guessed to the left. England in front but we're "on serve"

Ballack SCORES (England 2 – 2 Germany)

Germany's midfield maestro missed one in the group stages but it's a return to form here, waiting for Wright to commit before sending his shot in the opposite direction.

Gerrard SCORES (England 3 – 2 Germany)

I always feel the fourth penalty is crucial, and Steven Gerrard is a reliable man, going to the top right which Kahn can't get near despite going the right way.

Heinrich MISSES (England 3 – 2 Germany)

What!? Heinrich goes for power, leans back and finds the England fans behind the goal. England are at match point.

Ashley Cole SCORES (England 4 – 2 Germany)

Left footed, goal scoring machine Ashley Cole takes the perfect penalty that finds the side netting.

ENGLAND WIN 4-2 ON PENALTIES

Germany have lost a penalty shootout. To England. They'll never live that down. In my mind, the entire England squad does Andreas Moller's stupid walk that he did after scoring the winning penalty in Euro 96, but that's probably a bit petty. They all shook hands and had a jolly good knees up. England are in the semi-finals!!

The World Cup drama moves to Tokyo where France and Brazil play out a 0-0 draw, cancelling each other before finally being separated on the 9th round of penalties when Patrick Vieira scores and Fabien Barthez saves from Roque Junior. It's France next for England.

Poland are also in the semi-finals, beating Uruguay 3-1. Considering this is well before the days of Robert Lewandowski, Poland are very much surprise semi-finalists.

Czech Republic and Nigeria play out an unbelievable game in Seoul. Pavel Nedved gives the Czechs the lead but goals from Celestine Babayaro and Victor Ikpeba have Nigeria on the verge of the semi-finals. However, Lokvenc goes down under the challenge of goalkeeper Akanji in the 85th minute, and it's a penalty and a red card for the goalkeeper. Nedved scores the pen and sends it to extra time, which looks destined to end in a penalty shootout until West Ham's Tomas Repka scores in the 119th minute. It means we have only European teams in the last four.

France vs England – World Cup Semi-finals

We've bettered the real life performance, but as we're now two games from winning the World Cup, we might as well go for broke. This is the stage I was defeated in the last book and I felt genuinely crushed. Now it's my turn to seek revenge...on Sports Interactive.

France are managed by Roger Lemerre and he rocks the 4-4-2, though Robert Pires is out injured. As World Cup holders, they are rightfully an excellent team. We've seen how good Henry is from the season that has just passed, well now he has a lot of similarly talented friends rather than Francis Jeffers
.
France: Barthez, Thuram, Desailly, Silvestre, Candela, Carriere, Vieira, Dalmat, Micoud, Henry, Trezeguet. **Subs:** Lamouchi, Dutruel, Marlet, Djetou, Lizarazu, Djorkaeff, Wiltord

England are unchanged, though Joe Cole has joined the group of players one yellow away from a ban.

England: Wright, P Neville, Campbell, Ferdinand, Ash. Cole, Lampard, Beckham, J. Cole, Dyer, Scholes, Owen. **Subs:** Kirkland, Carragher, Southgate, Gerrard, Cole, Heskey, Fowler

Both nations belt out their national anthems. Rightly so, this opportunity doesn't come around that often.

KICK OFF – France get us underway. It will be neither team's last match regardless, as there's the much loved 3rd/4th place playoff to come.

5 mins – It's only 17 degrees in Pusan today, a massive drop from the 30 degrees England faced in Daegu.

10 mins – The first chance of a fairly turgid opening 10 minutes falls to England, but Michael Owen drags his shot wide.

15 mins – France have finally got going and they go close on two occasions here. Firstly, it's an Arsenal fest as Henry finds Vieira but his shot is pushed behind by Richard Wright, but he resulting corner from Dalmat is headed wide by Trezeguet. A let off.

21 mins – **YELLOW CARD**

Sol Campbell, what have you done? David Trezeguet is about 40 yards from goal on the right wing and he tries to knock the ball past big Sol. There's a tussle and Campbell pushes Trezeguet over. The referee awards a yellow card and it means England's ever present centre half will miss the final, should England get there. I imagine he will be less disappointed about missing the 3rd place playoff.

23 mins – **GOAL FOR ENGLAND! France 0 – 1 England (Joe Cole)**

Delirium for England and it's Joe Cole who grabs the opening goal. Dyer and Scholes link well, Scholes' fierce shot is spilled by club teammate Barthez and Joe Cole is onto the rebound quicker than anyone. He wheels away to the England bench, just the 67 minutes to hold out lads.

25 mins – England trying to stay calm but some of the younger players look like kids in a sweet shop. Paul Scholes does the universal symbol for calm down by moving his palms towards the ground. Nobody takes any notice.

31 mins – Kieron Dyer has been a revelation in this tournament, and here he is outrunning Mikael Silvestre before laying the ball off for Owen. His long range shot is poor though and goes well wide.

38 mins – I wonder what odds you would get on a Kieron Dyer header being the source of a goal in a World Cup semi-final? Whatever they are, they have drastically changed as the diminutive Newcastle man heads hopelessly over when well placed to meet Joe Cole's pinpoint centre.

42 mins – Off the bar! Paul Scholes was very quiet against Germany but he bursts into life here,

receiving a pass from Beckham, knocking the ball out of his feet and curling an effort that beats Barthez all ends up...but hits the crossbar. Silvestre clears. There's a knowing glance between Man Utd teammates, you can imagine that happens in training a lot.

43 mins – Beckham's corners are still delightful and this one is met by Campbell, but it goes well wide.

45 mins – Here's our first sight of Thierry Henry for a while, he spins away from Campbell on half way and that familiar long stride takes him towards the England box. He sets his sights but curls his shot well over the bar.

HALF TIME: France 0 – 1 England

So far, so good. England have got the important goal and had the better of the game generally. Thierry Henry has barely threatened.

KICK OFF – England get us back underway.

47 mins – Johan Micoud is an excellent player. He glides past Phil Neville and tries a shot from distance but Wright is down to get a glove on it and concedes the corner.

52 mins – **Substitution for France**. The largely anonymous David Trezeguet is off and replaced by Sylvain Wiltord.

55 mins – Nearly a second for England, but Barthez does brilliantly to save Michael Owen's low drive. From the resulting corner, Rio Ferdinand nearly gets onto a loose ball but Barthez is there again.

59 mins – **Substitution for France**. Carriere, who hasn't been much of a replacement for Robert Pires, is off and Sabri Lamouchi is on.

61 mins – Wiltord must equalise! No! Henry and Wiltord combine, Wiltord's volley is brilliantly saved but the rebound falls to the former Bordeaux man but Wright is up to make a second block. Incredible.

68 mins – Henry tries an effort from distance, but it's well wide. Not been his day so far.

73 mins – **Substitution for France**. Youri Djorkaeff is on for Micoud.

77 mins – A France corner comes to nothing. England have weathered the storm so far.

84 mins – **Substitution for England**. Steven Gerrard is on for Lampard. Nothing silly now and England will be in the World Cup final.

87 mins – France are pushing men forward and England nearly catch them on the break. Phil Neville breaks upfield and finds Dyer, who crosses to Scholes who takes the shot first time but it flies wide. He maybe had more time than he realised.

89 mins – **GOAL FOR ENGLAND! France 0 – 2 England (Steven Gerrard)**

What a goal to finish this game as a contest. France have been committing more and more men forward and England make them pay on the counter. David Beckham has the ball about 35 yards out and he spots the fresh legs of Steven Gerrard galloping into the box. Beckham pings a ball right on the money for Gerrard to strike on the volley without breaking stride, the volley goes low and hard past Barthez and England have done it! The final awaits.

90+2 mins – The game is still going on but nobody cares. Plans are already being made to be in Tokyo on Sunday. Joe Cole has a shot saved by Barthez.

FULL TIME: France 0 – 2 England

The talk begins of '66 cos they haven't found a cure. Maybe they just have. Joe Cole and Gerrard provide the antidote to a first World Cup final appearance in 36 years. And it's *only* Czech Republic or Poland. Oh my.

All eyes on Tokyo for the other semi-final, where a single goal from Marek Heinz leads the Czech Republic to the World Cup final. They made the Euro 96 final so I guess you can't say they are not without form since Czechoslovakia dissolved into Czech Republic and Slovakia. They have some exceptional players, most notably Pavel Nedved and Jan Koller and just because we've beaten some of the more fancied nations, they can't be taken lightly.

Before that though is the match we all came to see. The third/fourth place playoff is won by France, coming from 1-0 down to win 2-1 thanks to a late Sabri Lamouchi goal. Good for France, but Poland must be delighted with their World Cup efforts. And yes, the three of you who notice, this is a repeat of the 1982 3rd place match. But Poland won that one.

40,000 words leads us to this moment...

England vs Czech Republic – World Cup Final

In loving memory of Pavel Srnicek. RIP Pav, taken too soon. Pavel is a Geordie!

Is this the most unlikely final ever? Very few people would have picked this as the final when the tournament started, especially not after England's meek loss to Portugal and the almighty struggle against Ecuador. The Czech's have won 6 consecutive matches, including all three group games though you have to say the run of Japan, South Africa, Turkey, Costa Rica, Nigeria and Poland is one of the stranger paths to a World Cup final.

Unlikely or not, this is still the biggest game in world football. The Czechs have been serene throughout, whilst England have played themselves into form. That defeat against Portugal has been long forgotten, and this young team has come of age. There is only one player over the age of 30 in the starting 11, and that is Gareth Southgate. It's quite the time to make your first start of the tournament but with Sol Campbell suspended and Woodgate not 100% fit, Gareth and his experience has been given the nod. Yes, that experience includes missing a vital penalty at Euro 96, but these things are sent to try us. He might even manage England one day. But right now, he's got to hold this back four together.

England: Wright, P Neville, Southgate, Ferdinand, Ash. Cole, Lampard, Beckham, J. Cole, Dyer, Scholes, Owen. **Subs:** Kirkland, Carragher, Woodgate, Gerrard, Cole, Heskey, Fowler

The Czech team is pretty nifty, playing in a 4-4-2 diamond with Berger at the top behind Koller and Heinz. Nedved currently leads the race for the golden boot with 4 goals, but he is followed by his teammate Heinz on 3. Incidentally, Dyer, Lampard and Ashley Cole also all have 3.

Czech Republic: Srnicek, Votava, Repka, Fukal, Ujfalusi, Nikl, Nedved, Smicer, Heinz, Koller, Berger. **Subs:** Poborsky, Cerny, Ulich, Gabriel, Lokvenc, Jarolim, Baros

Of course several of the Czech team play in England, will that be an advantage? We're about to find out. The actual final was held in the International Stadium, Yokohama, but we're at a different venue here.

KICK OFF – The National Stadium in Tokyo is a cauldron of noise, over 61,000 fans are here for the 2002 World Cup final. England kick off.

2 mins – The Czech game plan is not subtle. Nedved sends a diagonal into the box towards big Jan Koller who towers above everyone but his powerful header is off target. An early warning.

7 mins – **GOAL FOR CZECH REPUBLIC! England 0 – 1 Czech Republic (Marek Heinz)**

England have made a nervous start and it seems very apparent that the Czech's have identified the aerially route as their best chance of victory. They take the lead when Votava comes marauding forward before hanging a cross up. Wright seems to hesitate for a second before coming off his line, giving Heinz the chance to get up ahead of him and head in. Not the start England wanted but the Czechs are obviously delighted.

9 mins – That put Heinz level with Nedved in the race for the golden boot. The England fans are still singing their hearts out, you feel this may be a once in a lifetime sort of thing.

11 mins – Off the post! So unlucky for Kieron Dyer, who goes on a mazy run before shooting from the edge of the box only to see his shot cannon back off the post.

14 mins – **GOAL FOR ENGLAND! England 1 – 1 Czech Republic (Kieron Dyer)**

England on terms! You feel it was important they got level pretty quickly after going behind. Scholes and Dyer have been a potent partnership in this tournament and they combine again, Scholes laying the ball off for Dyer to strike home – and what a strike! It arrows into the top corner giving Srnicek no chance. All to play for still.

18 mins – **GOAL FOR ENGLAND! England 2 – 1 Czech Republic (Michael Owen)**

England lead! Joe Cole is the architect, jinking past a few challenges to reach the edge of the box where he feeds in Michael Owen. Owen doesn't need a second invitation, steadying himself before passing the ball into the net beyond Srnicek. What a turnaround here in Tokyo!

20 mins – England rampant now, Dyer is again in the thick of the action but his shot is parried by Srnicek for a corner. Koller heads the corner away.

24 mins – Czech Republic try to respond, Koller and Heinz combining but Wright keeps out Heinz's header and smothers the loose ball before Nedved can get to it.

28 mins – Kieron Dyer is like a man possessed with winning the World Cup. This time his volley is

straight at Srnicek, much to the relief of the former Newcastle 'keeper.

31 mins – Richard Wright has had an exceptional tournament. Votava again goes forward and his cross finds Nikl, but his header is expertly kept out by Wright and it's hacked clear.

32 mins – **YELLOW CARD**

Ashley Cole is booked for holding back Patrik Berger, who had got goal side. I think that's called taking one for the team.

36 mins – **DISALLOWED GOAL**

England are very grateful to a World Cup final linesman for the second time in 36 years. Jan Koller thinks he has equalised but he has gone a yard too early and although his header is a peach, it is all for nothing.

38 mins – Koller shoots wide. He's not quite as good with his feet fortunately.

41 mins – Vladimir Smicer puts in a peach of a cross and it's Heinz on the end of it, but his header goes back across the face of goal. England need half time.

45 mins – Just as the fourth official indicates one added minute, Ashley and Joe Cole combine foen the left and Joe hits a shot that lacks power and Srnicek saves with ease. That'll be half time

HALF TIME: England 2 – 1 Czech Republic

45 minutes from history, fame, not being branded losers forever. Label it however you want, England might win the World Cup. It's been quite an even game, with 6 shots each, but England have been that little bit more accurate – though they are grateful the linesman was on his game in ruling out Koller's equaliser.

KICK OFF – Czech Republic restart the game, can they get back on terms?

48 mins – Pavel Nedved tries a curler but it's straight at Wright. At what time do we start keeping it in the corner?

51 mins – **YELLOW CARD**

Phil Neville is in the book after a late challenge on Smicer. Nedved's free kick is confidently claimed by Richard Wright.

56 mins – Joe Cole's still plugging away for England when he gets the chance. His cross finds Michael Owen but his header is well over the bar.

60 mins – Frank Lampard goes looking for his fourth goal of the tournament but his half volley flies a couple of yards wide. England are looking to kill this off.

64 mins – Dyer and Owen combine and Owen's shot is bound for the top corner until Srnicek sticks out a big paw and saves it. Repka clears but only as far as Joe Cole, but his shot is rushed and wild.

66 mins – **GOAL FOR ENGLAND! England 3 – 1 Czech Republic (Michael Owen)**

Breathing space! England 3-1 up now and surely now the World Cup is coming home. Joe Cole again the provider, feeding Owen who spins his marker and shoots low and hard across Srnicek and the ball cannons in off the far post. Delightful!

68 mins – There's a party in the England end. The crosses of St George are flying all around, football is coming home.

71 mins – Czech Republic still trying to muster a response, Votava's corner finds its way to Patrik

Berger but his effort is miles over the bar. Ironic cheers from one end, glum faces at the other.

73 mins – Smicer is the latest to be denied by Richard Wright, it's another top save as well, low down to his right hand side.

77 mins – **YELLOW CARD**

Joe Cole has been a nuisance all day and he is nearly cut in two by his club colleague Tomas Repka. It's a yellow card but it could have been red.

78 mins – **Substitution for England.** Phil Neville is off and Jamie Carragher is on. Neville is on a yellow card so it looks like a safety first approach for the closing minutes.

81 mins – England keeping the ball, trying to see out time.

85 mins – Lampard is one away from being level at the top of the scoring charts but this effort from about 35 yards is ambitious to say the least. Srnicek pats it down.

89 mins – **Substitution for Czech Republic.** Jan Koller has given everything but he is replaced by Vratislav Lokvenc for the closing moments.

90 mins – 3 added minutes. The England bench are ready to celebrate.

**FULL TIME: England 3 – 1 Czech Republic
ENGLAND WIN THE 2002 WORLD CUP**

This was how it was meant to be! England players, fans and management celebrating in the Tokyo night, 36 years of hurt behind them and a bright future ahead. What went wrong?

Before I go…

Whilst I'll leave you to imagine the fictional celebrations, there are some awards to hand out. The team of the tournament has presumably been selected by Roy Hodgson, as only Joe Cole features from my all conquering England team. He's on the left of a midfield four that includes Mendieta on the right and a dynamic central duo of Samuel Eto'o and Sun Jihai. Well, why not?

The Golden Boot goes to Marek Heinz, he's ahead of Pavel Nedved despite both getting four. I don't know how they decided to separate them. A funny story about Nedved, it seems Juventus had a terrible season in Serie A and came 9th, so they entered the Inter-Toto cup. 6 days after losing the World Cup final he played and scored a last minute goal as Juventus won 1-0 away to AEK Larnaca of Cyprus.

Kieron Dyer and Joe Cole both finished top assisters with four apiece. Dyer signed a new contract with Newcastle on £70k a week, but Joe Cole "feels he needs to leave (West Ham) to further his career" which is no surprise considering he finished the World Cup with an average rating of 8.57.

So, whilst England can rightly be delighted at how they have outperformed their real life counterparts, Arsenal are our big losers, going from double winners to…nothing winners. Man Utd retained their Premier League crown but failed to make much of a mark in Europe, where Real Madrid failed to win the Champions Leagye and Zidane's marvellous volley never happened. Lazio are the surprise benefactors there, whilst Feyenoord didn't even come close to winning the UEFA Cup. Shakhtar Donetsk were somewhat surprising winners. Leicester are the big overachievers, they'll have European football next season after finishing 6th whilst Sunderland can be happy with 8th over their actual finishing position of 17th. West Ham drop from 7th to 14th, Aston Villa from 8th to 15th, and Tottenham 9th to 16th in a bad season for the clubs who had been chasing European football. Celtic replicated their real life dominance of the SPL, though the in game version couldn't quite rack up 103 points. Don't get me started on Spain. It was all wrong.

But that's it from me, you now know exactly how the 2001/02 season would have played out if Championship Manager 01/02 was calling the shots. I know which storyline I prefer.

If you enjoyed this book, you will love...

"The World According to Championship Manager 97/98" by David Black

"Johnny Cooper, Championship Manager: The Story of Mansfield Town according to Championship Manager 99/00" by Chris Darwen

And

"Johnny Cooper, Championship Manager: The Second Season Syndrome" by Chris Darwen

All the books are available in print and digitally from Amazon.

Printed in Great Britain
by Amazon